Following Egeria

A Modern Pilgrim in the Holy Land

LAWRENCE R. FARLEY

ANCIENT FAITH PUBLISHING
CHESTERTON, INDIANA

Following Egeria: A Modern Pilgrim in the Holy Land
© 2014 Lawrence R. Farley

All rights reserved.

Scripture quotations are taken from the New King James Version,
© 1979, 1980, 1982 by Thomas Nelson, Inc. Used by permission.

Published by:
    Ancient Faith Publishing
    A Division of Ancient Faith Ministries
    P.O. Box 748
    Chesterton, IN 46304

ISBN: 978-1-936270-21-7

Cover design by Symbology Creative

Printed in the United States of America

25 24 23 22 21 20 19   13 12 11 10 9 8 7 6 5 4 3 2

*Dedicated to
Deacon Gregory Wright,
best of traveling companions,
whose kindness brought me
to the Holy Land*

Contents

Introduction: Following Egeria ❧ 7

1: Traveling to Jerusalem ❧ 15

2: Jerusalem ❧ 25

3: The Mount of Olives ❧ 43

4: Bethlehem and Judea ❧ 65

5: Bethany and Wadi Qelt ❧ 83

6: Outside the Walls: St. Stephen's & Siloam ❧ 97

7: Galilee ❧ 109

8: Recovering the Via Dolorosa ❧ 139

9: The Temple and Its Area ❧ 153

Conclusion: Retaining the Rock ❧ 169

Materials Consulted ❧ 181

INTRODUCTION

Following Egeria

Loving ladies, light of my heart, this [Constantinople] is where I am writing to you. My present plan is, in the Name of Christ our God, to travel to Asia. If after that I am still alive, and able to visit further places, I will either tell you about them face to face (if God so wills), or at any rate write to you about them if my plans change. In any case, ladies, light of my heart, whether I am "in the body" or "out of the body," please do not forget me.

— EGERIA, WRITING TO HER MONASTIC
COMMUNITY DURING HER TRAVELS

In May of 2013, I visited the Holy Land, traveling with my friend Gregory Wright, who serves with me as a deacon in my parish of St. Herman of Alaska Orthodox Church in Langley, BC, Canada. We arrived in the Holy Land on May 10 and left soon after, on May 20. As we walked the crazy and ancient cobblestones of the Old City and breathlessly visited sites such as Nazareth, Capernaum, Bethlehem, and Jericho, we had as our guide a copy of the travel book for Israel and the Palestinian Territories published by Lonely Planet. It was a good enough guidebook. But I felt a greater kinship and link with a more ancient document, one representing not the thoughts of the writers for Lonely Planet, but those of a Christian woman who lived over 1600 years ago. Her name, from what we can figure out, was Egeria.

For the longest time scholars were not even sure of her name. She made a tour like ours of the holy places between AD 381 and 384. (Thus her trip took considerably longer than ten days.) She wrote about all that she saw and experienced, making copious notes for her "sisters" back home. The problem is that the first part of her book was lost, so that the text now opens with the words, "biblical sites were pointed out. In the meanwhile we were walking along between the mountains and came to a spot where they opened out to form an endless valley."

The last part of the book is missing too, so that it ends with the words, "On the first and second days they assemble in the Great Church, the Martyrium, on the third day in the Eleona Church on the Mount from which the Lord ascended into heaven after His passion (I mean the church which contains the cave where the Lord taught the apostles on the Mount of Olives). On the fourth day . . ." That's it. It ends there, so that we have no idea what she was about to tell us about the fourth day.

We therefore have neither the beginning nor the end of the book, and so we can only guess about her name, her home, who her "sisters" were, or how the travelogue ends. Presently the scholarly smart money gives her name as Egeria (previously scholars thought her name might be Aetheria or Sylvia) and suggests that she came from a community of nuns in Spain. She herself told the bishop of Edessa that she came "right from the other end of the earth" (which impressed him no end), and Spain is as a good a guess as any.

But despite these lacunae in our knowledge, her personality shines through her writing clearly enough. She wanted to see and know everything, to stand where the saints once stood, to touch places that once knew the Lord's presence. She was hungry to see and experience absolutely everything. For her this long trek was the dream and journey of a lifetime, and she didn't want to waste a minute. I rather liked her and thought I knew exactly how she felt. I felt myself to be following in her footsteps and copying her agenda, even if I visited only a fraction of the places she did. Like her, I also made copious notes, and unlike her, took many photos.

The world in which Egeria walked is long gone. The world of the fourth century was a world newly baptized. Prior to that time, things were dark indeed for the Christians of the Roman

Empire, for the threat of persecution and death hung over their heads like the sword of Damocles, even though their growth in numbers meant that immediately prior to Constantine they constituted (according to some modern guesses) about a tenth of the empire.

Then suddenly and miraculously, everything changed. The so-called Edict of Milan in 313 under the Emperor Constantine allowed Christians the freedom to exist and to own property, and they came out of the catacombs (metaphorically speaking; they never did really worship in the catacombs), wondering and blinking in the light of a new day. The emperor favored them and was prepared to open the largesse of the imperial treasury to prove it and to build churches. Large ones.

Led by St. Helen, construction soon began in Palestine, as Constantine's men discovered the location of holy places through the historical memories and stories handed down by the local people who preserved such things as part of their family tradition. Imperial engineers built big basilicas to mark those sacred spots and facilitate Christian devotion there. Large churches went up in Bethlehem, in Jerusalem, and elsewhere. Indeed, throughout the Roman Empire, Christians came out of proverbial hiding and spoke with new confidence—a confidence that came from knowing the emperor was now on their side.

Some thought the whole thing was too good to last and that everything would soon blow over (the Emperor Julian's hostility to Christ "the Galilean" seemed for the moment to prove this).

Introduction

But it was not to be. Rather, the favor of Constantine proved to be the wave of the future, so that for centuries to come, the Roman Empire would be a Christian empire. Pagan Rome had become Christian Byzantium, and would remain so—at least in spots—for about a thousand years.

Egeria lived and traveled and wrote at the very beginning of this new day, and she traveled throughout the empire confident that she would find a welcome by hospitable bishops everywhere, bishops who delighted to welcome pilgrims like her and who exulted in the new ascendancy of the Christian Faith. Churches were everywhere, and it was a good time to be a Christian.

As time progressed, of course, things occurred in the world that Egeria and the bishops who welcomed her could not have imagined—things like the explosive growth of Islam in the seventh century. This meant that much of the Christian world Egeria knew would be covered over by another layer, an Islamic one, as Islam conquered much of the Roman Empire and turned churches into mosques.

Then came the countercharge of the Crusaders, valiantly pushing back after hundreds of years of Muslim pushing and conquest. (Within a century from the death of Mohammed, the Muslims had expanded their empire as far as north-central France, only being repelled from there at the Battle of Tours by Charles Martel in 732.) For a while, a Christian Crusader layer overlaid the Islamic one. Then the Crusaders' influence in the Holy Land was broken at the Horns of Hattin in Palestine in 1187. After that came the Ottoman Empire, and then the European ascendancy, culminating in the British Mandate over the fate of Palestine. And then, in 1948, came the establishment of the State of Israel.

The point of all this history for modern pilgrims is this: Much of the Christian world Egeria knew lies buried in the Holy Land, recoverable now only through archeology and historical research. Pious Christian devotion asks questions and demands answers to many things for which definitive answers cannot be given: Where was the Theotokos born? Where did she die? What was the exact spot from which Christ ascended into heaven? Piety wants to know, and there are now, as in the days of Egeria, no shortage of guides giving answers with the assurance popular piety demands.

But thoughtful and thorough scholars today are not as confident as the guides and speak with less assurance. Some pilgrims prefer the confidence of the guides. I prefer the scholars, even if they do speak more tentatively. I traveled to the Holy Land in the resounding footsteps of Egeria, seeing the guides but listening to the scholars, and offering prayer in the holy places for myself and for those I love.

The result of all that travel, reading, and prayer is the present book. Unlike Egeria's, my aim was not simply to log my experiences as a diary, nor to produce yet another guidebook. And my aim was certainly not to record my personal feelings and devotion (of which rather little will appear in this book, abundant

Introduction

though they may have been during my time there). Rather, my aim is to produce an extended meditation, part travelogue, part historical and archeological guesswork, a tiny bit of political commentary, and much theological reflection. It is offered as an advance preparation and resource for those going to the Holy Land to see the sacred sites for themselves, and also as spiritual and theological fruit of the trip to those who will never get to go there.

My limitations in carrying out this aim are obvious enough, and I hereby own up to them at the outset: I am not a professional historian or an archeologist, and so am dependent upon the works of others as I try to figure it all out for myself. But I hope that what the book lacks in professional expertise, it makes up for in the vividness that comes from a pilgrim's hungry heart. After all, like Egeria before me, I was there. And like her, I hope that by reading these meditations, you may experience something of what I did when I fulfilled the dream of a lifetime and walked in the holy places, seeking echoes of a sacred past and finding the enduring presence of the living God.

~ I ~

Traveling to Jerusalem

From Tathis we went by the way I already knew, and arrived at Pelusium. And from there we went on through all the Egyptian staging-posts of our outward journey till we reached the frontier of Palestine. And from there, in the Name of Christ our God, I returned after several staging-posts in Palestine to Aelia, which is Jerusalem.

EGERIA, CHAPTER 9 IN HER TRAVELOGUE,
DESCRIBING HER JOURNEY TO JERUSALEM

It took us two days to reach the Holy Land, traveling from Vancouver to Tel Aviv, with changes of plane in London and

Zurich. By the time we arrived, we had been awake about forty-eight hours. The trip for me had its own peculiar rigors, since I had injured my back just days before departure, so that my therapist advised me to stand and not sit for the duration of the plane trip. (I sat anyway.)

I detail these slight inconveniences to contrast them with what travel to the Holy Land meant to our ancestors. For them, pilgrimage involved not just interminable sitting in a plane where legroom was apparently restricted to Executive Class, or long layovers in airports between flights, or jet-lagged fatigue. For them pilgrimage was lengthy, arduous, and dangerous to life and limb—as well as hideously expensive. Pilgrims routinely made their wills before they departed from their homes, realizing there was a good chance they might not return. Travelers were subject to robbery, kidnapping, disease, death on the high seas, and death at the hands of brigands.

St. Paul's litany of dangers in 2 Corinthians 11:25–26 ("in perils of waters, in perils of robbers, . . . in perils in the city, in perils in the wilderness, in perils in the sea") found abundant echo in the experiences of all who went on pilgrimage. Pilgrims went about in groups and armed. They prayed their way from home to the Holy Land, and not just because of their tremendous piety. All travel was dangerous in those days. It is not for nothing that the Church has always included in its litanies prayers for "those who travel by land and by sea."

Pilgrimage in those days thus was itself a kind of *podvig*, an

Traveling to Jerusalem

ascetic exploit. It was not for the faint of heart or for those who, like Bilbo in *The Hobbit*, wanted to avoid adventures because they made one late for dinner. Pilgrimage was difficult, and it was these very difficulties that could purify the heart, so that one arrived at one's destination inwardly prepared to venerate the holy places. The ancients felt all temples should be hard to access so that one's difficulties ensured that one entered the temple with a pure heart, and ancient pilgrims abundantly fulfilled this precept. The difficulties and sufferings experienced along the way worked their spiritual alchemy, heightening a desire for the holy, sharpening spiritual hunger. One fasted from the routine and safe to come at last to one's destination as if one were coming to a sacrament.

Of course no one today wants to duplicate this rigorous experience of the earlier pilgrims or increase the difficulties and dangers of modern travel. But we can learn from their experience not to complain about the minor inconveniences of travel today. Our aim is to become less the air-conditioned tourist and more the devout pilgrim, daring and enduring all things to reach our holy destination.

Not all people in the ancient world thought the dangers and rigors of travel were worth it. St. Gregory of Nyssa, brother of St. Basil the Great and famous among the Cappadocian Fathers, thought pilgrimage a bad idea, if only because of the moral temptations that beset the traveler. In a letter now called *On Pilgrimages*, he writes to a fellow ascetic about whether or not those seeking a life of holiness should "make it a part of their devotion to behold those spots at Jerusalem where the memorials of our Lord's life in the flesh are on view." He thought they should not make it an obligatory part of their devotion.

St. Gregory begins by noting that "when the Lord invites the blessed to their inheritance in the Kingdom of heaven [in Matt. 25:31–40] He does not include a pilgrimage to Jerusalem among their good works," and he calls attention to the fact that such travel inevitably involves use of "inns and hostelries and cities of the East [which] present many examples of license and indifference to vice." Moreover, Gregory asks his would-be pilgrim, "What advantage is reaped by him who reaches those celebrated spots themselves? He cannot imagine that our Lord is living in the body there at the present day." Is it because the pilgrim thinks attaining holiness is easier there? Hardly, for "if the divine grace was more abundant around Jerusalem than elsewhere, sin would not be so much the fashion among those that live there, but as it is, there is no form of uncleanness that is not perpetrated among them," and he gives a list. He concludes that his faith in Christ "was not increased afterwards any more" by the pilgrimage he once took there, and he draws the moral (hard to deny) that "change of place does not effect any drawing nearer to God."

It is hard to refute the brother of St. Basil. Yet all this means is that pilgrimage is not necessary to Christian growth and faith (as it is necessary to Muslims, who are required to make a pilgrimage to Mecca once in their lifetime if they possibly can). Having made the pilgrimage myself, I would agree with Egeria and countless pilgrims before me that although not, strictly speaking, necessary, "beholding the spots at Jerusalem where the memorials of our Lord's life in the flesh are on view" was a tremendous blessing. It did not in itself make me more holy (Gregory of Nyssa was right about that), but it did help establish a connection in mind and emotion between the things I had been reading about in the Bible my whole adult life and the historical realities themselves.

This is because the human heart instinctively seeks to build bridges, especially bridges to the past. We live in a world of time and space. The river of time only flows in one direction, and as Joni Mitchell famously reminded us in her song "The Circle Game," "we can't return; we can only look behind at where we came." This makes that backward look even more important and the memories that constitute that look even more precious.

Yet in our own lives, memory fails and distorts, and sometimes the only unfading connections we have with our own precious past are photos and keepsakes. In the case of history, and especially sacred biblical history, the only connections for most of us are the records of history, whether written in the Bible or in secular texts. And, as with our own personal pasts, we find that mere words do not satisfy us enough; they do not make a secure enough bridge. We want a connection with the biblical past, and if we cannot build that bridge through time, we must therefore seek to build it through space.

That is, we seek to return to the actual places where those sacred events happened, "the spots where the memorials of our Lord's life are on view," to use the words of Gregory of Nyssa. We long to connect with those sacred events—to actually see our Lord as He hung on the cross, to be physically present at the empty tomb on the first Paschal morning and to hear the words of the angel, "He is risen; He is not here; behold the place where they laid Him" (Mark 16:6).

Since we cannot travel through time to Golgotha and the garden tomb, we long at least to be present at those places, to touch the wood of the cross or the rock of Golgotha where the cross stood, or to enter into the tomb and to kiss that sacred space on which the Lord's body once lay. Or, at the very least, to stand in the actual spot, the authentic site, and to know that on this approximate patch of ground, on this bit of terrestrial real estate, the incarnate God lived and spoke and died and rose.

Since we cannot travel through time, we attempt to travel through space to connect with the places where these things happened. Gregory's cautions notwithstanding, the desire to connect with the past through pilgrimage runs strong in the Christian, and from the earliest days countless believers have braved dangers to travel to the Holy Land and feed the hunger of their hearts by connecting with the Lord at the holy places.

For me, the epicenter of all this geographical sanctity was

Jerusalem. Throughout the long years of Christian history, Jerusalem has been more than a city. It has been a hope. There is an epitaph carved on the grave of a Christian woman who lived in fourth-century Asia Minor. It reads, "Here sleeps the blessed Chione, who has found Jerusalem for she prayed much." No doubt this otherwise unknown peasant woman was much loved by those who saw her die and who buried her and carved this little epitaph. And when they came to write a few words that would outlive them all and be a fitting tribute to their beloved Chione, they could think of nothing better than Jerusalem. For them as for Christians before and after, finding Jerusalem was the goal of all their existence.

That is a lot of weight for any earthly city to bear, especially a city so tiny as Jerusalem has been for most of its history. Like all places in the Middle East, it has a long history. In the days of Abraham, the king of the city was Melchizedek (we would probably think of him today as more like a mayor). In David's day, the city was still a Canaanite stronghold called Jebus when he conquered it and made it his own. Like many places in the Holy Land back then, it was small, consisting of only about ten acres that ran south of the modern city walls, with a population that did not exceed a thousand people. It was enlarged when David built the temple complex north of the original city, and enlarged again under Hezekiah, who built it westward. Until 1860, Jerusalem was more or less confined to what we today call "the Old City," an area of only about 0.35 square miles, or

224 acres. Yet despite its compact size, from the days of David onward, Jerusalem has been the bearer of hopes and dreams.

That is because David decided, in a flash of political genius, to bring the ark of God there, so that all Israel would have to come to his city when they came to worship God at the only shrine He authorized. At a stroke David united the political life of Israel with its religious life, making the City of David also the City of God. Psalm after psalm celebrated God's dwelling in David's city—or Zion (meaning "height"), as it was usually called. God had blessed Zion, acquiescing in the move to David's city. He had Himself "chosen Zion; / He has desired it for His dwelling place: / 'This is My resting place forever; / Here I will dwell, for I have desired it. / I will abundantly bless her provision; / I will satisfy her poor with bread'" (Ps. 132:13–15).

Davidic Jerusalem was now "the city of our God . . . the joy of all the earth" (Ps. 48:1–2). It was "the perfection of beauty," out of which "God will shine forth" (Ps. 50:2). And it was not only the psalmists who spoke thus; the prophets also celebrated Jerusalem as the dwelling place of God, the center of the earth. "Out of Zion shall go forth the law, / And the word of the LORD from Jerusalem" (Is. 2:3). All hopes were fixed upon her; after the catastrophic fall of the city to the invading Babylonians in 586 BC and the years of exile, God promised, "I am again returning to Jerusalem with mercy; . . . The Lord will again comfort Zion, and will again choose Jerusalem" (Zech. 1:16–17). So powerfully would God dwell in His chosen city that it would have a new name: "Yahweh-shammah"—"the Lord *is* there" (Ezek. 48:35).

For the Christian, all these hopes were fulfilled in Jesus and His Church, for it was out of His Church in Jerusalem that the law and the word of the Lord went forth after the Day of Pentecost. Christ foretold it and claimed the promises of the city for Himself: "Thus it is written, . . . that repentance and forgiveness of sins should be preached in [My] name to all nations, beginning at Jerusalem" (Luke 24:46–47).

The hopes revolving around the earthly Zion coalesced through Christ into a hope in the heavenly Zion. The Kingdom Christ brought was too mighty to be sustained through any earthly nation or sovereignty. It was an eschatological reality, a Kingdom "not of this world" (John 18:36). Earthly Jerusalem, like all the cities of the world, might rise or fall, but the Kingdom of God would endure.

Even before Jerusalem fell to the Roman power in AD 70 and was essentially wiped off the earth as a city (the new city was renamed "Aelia" by the Romans), Christians knew that their true Jerusalem was the heavenly and eternal one. Even when the apostles still made their headquarters in a Jerusalem suburb and when Jerusalem was still the mother church, Paul could write, "the Jerusalem above is free, . . . the mother of us all" (Gal. 4:26).

In our hearts are the highways to Zion, and our feet long to stand within her gates (Ps. 84:5; 122:2). And as for blessed Chione, the Jerusalem we long to find is the heavenly one, the true city of the great King, where Christ our Lord sits at the right hand of God. Entering the earthly Jerusalem has been for Christian pilgrims like tasting a sacrament: the outward bread is the city in the land of Palestine; the true and saving Bread is the Kingdom of God. The earthly Jerusalem shines because it bears the weight of sacred history and because it points away from itself toward eternity.

So it was that when my traveling companion and I touched down in Tel Aviv in the wee hours of the morning and took a taxi to Jerusalem, we arrived like men in a dream. And when we left our apartment a few sleepless hours later to enter the Old City, I found that nothing I had read had prepared me for my first sight of its ancient walls.

We walked through a modern street mall, full of expensive shops with signs mostly in English, a retail lane that could have been in any Western city. We exited the lane and abruptly came upon those ancient walls, which reared up before us. I felt as if I had traveled back in time and stepped suddenly from my own twenty-first century into Herodian Jerusalem. I stopped, and stared, and wondered. The sight of those walls affected me as if they were a mountain.

~: 2 :~

Jerusalem

Loving sisters, I am sure it will interest you to know about the daily services they have in the holy places, and I must tell you about them. All the doors of the Anastasis [the Church of the Resurrection, or the Holy Sepulcher] are opened before cockcrow each day, and the monks and virgins come in, and also some lay men and women, at least those who are willing to wake at such an hour.... As soon as dawn comes, they start the morning hymns and the bishop with his clergy comes and joins them. He goes straight into the cave, into the railed area.

EGERIA, CHAPTER 24, DESCRIBING
THE DAILY SERVICES IN THE
CHURCH OF THE HOLY SEPULCHER

The Church of the Holy Sepulcher

*I*n the early hours of the breaking day, as a first order of business after dropping our luggage at the rented apartment, my companion and I made our way to the Church of the Holy Sepulcher. It was about 7:00 AM, with few others up and working in the shops that lined the winding streets of the Old City, so we made a peaceful journey. (A journey later in the day would bring a barrage of unsolicited calls for attention from the vendors we passed—a process my companion referred to as being "heckled and shekeled.") We entered the city at the Jaffa Gate (so called because it anciently led out of Jerusalem toward the city of Jaffa, or Joppa) and plunged into the winding maze of intersecting lanes, one of which led to the church. When we saw St. Helena's Road, we turned right and quickly found ourselves in the large courtyard before the doors of the church. One of the doorways had been bricked up, so we entered through the only remaining one and found ourselves standing in the holiest place in the world.

Immediately in front of us lay a large marble slab, called the Stone of Anointing, because it commemorates the place where our Lord was laid after He was taken down from the Cross and anointed in preparation for burial. (It is not the first slab laid there to mark the spot; previously laid stones had been worn away through the years by the kisses of devout pilgrims and had to be replaced. This latest slab was laid in 1810.) People were prostrating themselves on the slab and kissing it. They were also spreading out cloths upon the stone, and we soon discovered why—the stone was fragrant with myrrh, and the cloths were placed upon it to soak up some of the miraculously flowing liquid.

Myrrh often flows from it, especially during Holy Week. The myrrh is, I thought, the Lord's provision for His people who come to this holy place in faith to find grace and blessing. Other sites are of historical interest, certainly, and are places where one can pour out the heart in prayer. But here God pours out something in return. Here grace flows, making the souls of seekers fragrant with the scent of heaven. I joined the other pilgrims in venerating the sacred stone the church had laid here, prayerfully placing my priest's stole on the fragrant myrrh.

We then turned back and to the right. Immediately upon entering the main doors, one finds a stairway under an arch leading up the rock of Golgotha.

As we approached it, I walked up the steep steps in a kind of trembling awe, for I had come halfway across the globe to find this place. There are two chapels at the top of the stairs: a Roman Catholic one on the right, marking the place where Christ was nailed to the cross, and the Orthodox one on the left, marking the actual place where the cross was erected and where Christ hung and died for the salvation of the world. Under the altar over that very spot is a silver disk in the floor. Those visiting the site bow low under the altar to place their hand through a hole in the disk to touch the rock that held the cross.

A few people were there even at this early hour, including a ponytailed Orthodox priest in a cassock, kneeling and weeping in joy. He covered his face with his hand, so as not to be a spectacle, and stayed there until he could recover himself. He pictured in his mind how this all had looked two thousand years ago—a small hill, covered then with earth and dirt, its small summit approachable by a more gentle incline. He saw the Roman soldiers and the Lord, staggering under the weight of the crossbeam He carried up through the streets and up that slope. He saw the three crosses and the crowds. Maybe not exactly here, where the Orthodox altar stands, but anyway within a few yards of it, Christ hung and suffered and died. The priest bowed low and prostrated himself before the inner vision. This moment was the fulfillment of his life's dream, dividing his life into two unequal halves.

When my diaconal companion and I finally and reluctantly left that place, we descended another flight of stairs to find another chapel at the bottom of the rock of Golgotha. It is the original base of the rock and is now called the Chapel of Adam, recalling the story that Adam was buried there and that Christ's blood, flowing down the rock, cleansed Adam from sin and death. The fissure in the rock is pointed out by guides as being made by the earthquake that occurred at the time of Christ's death (Matt. 27:51). In fact, geologists suggest that the fissure was there before Christ's death, and that its presence in the rock was the reason the rock was left standing there in the first place. The other rocks in the same area had been quarried and taken away for use in building; this outcrop of rock was left untouched because the fissure in it rendered it useless to the builders looking for good stone. For me the principal interest in the chapel was that it showed something of the original size and dimensions of the hill on which Christ died.

In another part of the rambling church, down some steps, is the chapel of St. Helen. It marks the place of the original cistern where Constantine's engineers and builders found the crosses the Romans used on Golgotha. The Church was in fact dotted with little chapels (in good medieval Crusader fashion), each one preserving something of the original landscape as it was before the Constantinian building began.

We turned then to the so-called Edicule (from the Latin *aediculum*, or "little building"), the place containing the original tomb of Christ. It is now a large and impressive structure, adorned, as is everything else there, with all the splendor and finery of which later ages were capable. It consists of two places: the outer "chapel of the angels," the outer part of the original tomb where the women first met the angel who told them of Christ's Resurrection (Mark 16:5), and the inner chamber itself, containing the bench where the body of Jesus was placed. This is now overlaid with a marble slab and hung with many lamps. The lineup to enter the Edicule was impressive and began to form before entry was granted at 9:00 AM. As I looked up at the Edicule, I felt a sense of spiritual vertigo, as if I were standing at the heart of the world, the epicenter from which radiates all subsequent Christian sanctity.

As I lined up and moved forward in the queue, I had time to think about where I was and what it was like before. Two thousand years ago, the place where I was standing was in a garden, just outside the city walls, and open to the sky. All has now been enclosed and decorated with what to many visitors is gaudy Byzantine frippery. For many, perhaps, the contrast between the simple garden tomb of the Gospel story and the elaborate architectural enclosure of the present church is too much for their pious historical imagination to bear. But I was used to Byzantine standards of ornament, and for me the power of the place lay not in its outward similarity to how it originally looked, but in its geographical authenticity. For here, in this very spot, Christ's dead body was laid, and from this very spot He rose from the dead.

The Tomb is very small (as one would expect a tomb to be), and only four people can enter at one time. The monk presiding over the queue does not allow the visitors much time in the Tomb itself, since his thankless task is to hurry everyone through so that each visitor may spend at least a little time there. When my own turn came, I knelt to kiss the marble slab placed over the original tomb bed and quietly chanted the Paschal troparion, "Christ is risen from the dead, trampling down death by death and upon those in the tombs bestowing life." It was all over in less than a minute (the one tasked with keeping the line moving was very efficient), but the power of the place was not affected by the shortness of the time I was allowed there. It was as if the very air there still held echoes of the moment of Christ's Resurrection.

The holy places of Golgotha and the Edicule have undergone considerable change throughout the years. Constantine built a wonderful church on the original sites, which was reduced to rubble in 1009 by the "mad Caliph" Hakim. Emperor Monomachos did his best to restore it in 1048, but ran out of funds and so could only restore it partially, not to its original grand scale. The Crusaders coming afterward made their architectural contribution, beginning work in 1112, using their customary Romanesque style of architecture and roofing over spaces that were once open to the sky. Yet as I stood and stared, I could see how it looked before, in its original state and then as it was when Constantine beautified it in the fourth century. I looked about and saw how things were in centuries past—not through a vision, but through something more important to authentic living than supernatural vision—through imagination.

In the first century, as said above, all this was open country. The walls of the city were differently positioned then. Herod Agrippa altered the walls in AD 44, and in 135 the Emperor Hadrian changed things still further. During the time of Jesus, the present site of the Holy Sepulcher lay just outside the city walls. Golgotha was not a large hill or mountain (as sometimes portrayed in Christian art), but rather a crag or hillock, a raised outcropping of rock reached by a slight incline, whose top afforded maximum visibility so that all passing by could see what happened to those who defied the Roman power.

At the foot of the crag lay a garden, a place outside the city where Jewish tombs were carved from the caves. Joseph of Arimathea had his own tomb there, a few meters from the crag where Christ was executed. The tombs were of the basic Jewish type, with an antechamber in which the body was laid out in preparation for burial and an inner chamber in which the prepared body was finally laid. Stones would be set in front of the outer door to prevent animals from coming in and ravaging the bodies. Nearby were cisterns.

No doubt local Christians of the first centuries went there privately to feed their piety and to pray, much as Christians have done ever since. Certainly a local site of such importance to Christians would not be forgotten, but the spot would remain in the family histories of Christians living in and near Jerusalem, passed down by word of mouth from generation to generation, from father to son. Finding the actual spot would not have been difficult; after all, large crags outside city walls with tombs nearby do not move and are hard to miss.

The Romans destroyed Jerusalem in AD 70 under Titus, and launched another assault in 135 under Hadrian, who razed the city and built another city there in its place, named Aelia

Capitolina (named in part after himself, Aelius). It seems he took steps to dissuade Christians from coming to the site, for he brought in a large amount of earth to cover the place and make it level, paved it over with stone, and then built a temple to Jupiter Capitolinus and placed a statue of Venus there. There it all sat, covering up the Christian site—but also marking it, with the unintended result that others could later be sure the original Christian site was located here. Eusebius, writing in the mid-fourth century, decried its pre-Constantinian state as "a gloomy shrine of lifeless idols."

But it would not so remain. When Constantine decided, with his mother, Helena, to honor the Christian Faith by building a church over the site of the cross and the empty tomb, he began to renovate in earnest. His engineers worked to clear away the earth his pagan predecessor had brought in, demolishing the stone pavement and the temples and exposing the Jewish tombs beneath them.

We may perhaps gather some hint of how the original tombs may have looked from looking at the presently unadorned tombs near the present Tomb of Christ. These tombs, now known as the tombs of Joseph of Arimathea and Nicodemus, can be found a little behind the Edicule. They are not very prominent, and I suspect many pilgrims miss them, for there is little to advertise their presence or to distinguish them. But they drew me in nonetheless, for I thought I could see in their unadorned simplicity something of the original state of our Lord's own tomb when it was first found by Constantine's engineers many centuries ago.

Work then began on the new Christian site. The place of the Lord's tomb was chiseled away so that its double chambers stood in a small rock cave, now isolated from the other tombs and standing alone in a courtyard open to the sky with a small building built over it to enshrine it, surrounded by columns. A forecourt stood before it, and a few meters from the Tomb the crag of Golgotha, about twelve feet high. The crag seems to have been reduced in lateral size by the imperial engineers so as to fit into the new Constantinian complex: rather than a crag whose top could be approached by climbing a gentle slope, it was now chiseled down to become a more formidable projection. It was now not a gently sloping incline, but a crag whose top could not be easily climbed without the aid of steep stairs. The rock remained in the church complex as a memorial of our Lord's Passion, marking the actual place where the cross once stood.

Behind the forecourt that held the crag of Golgotha and the Tomb was the actual church, the so-called Martyrium, with its long colonnaded nave stretching back a long way. Behind the nave was the entry court of the church itself, open to the sky. It was all large and lofty—much larger and loftier than the present structure—with rows of double colonnades. Thus it stood when dedicated in 335. By 348, further changes were made, and the Tomb was enclosed by a rotunda, called appropriately enough the Anastasis, or the Resurrection. This is how it looked when Egeria visited it some years later.

As mentioned above, many changes took place after the Byzantine church had been completed by the middle of the fourth century—invasion, destruction, burning, and desolation caused by Persian and Muslim in turn. The present building bears little resemblance to its Constantinian original. And perhaps the greatest difference between the two structures is this: In the days of the fourth century, when Egeria visited the site, it was a working parish church. Its pastor, the bishop of Jerusalem, offered a schedule of services to his local flock, preached to a stable and continuing community, catechized catechumens and then baptized them, and presided over a parish like all the other parishes of the Roman world—save that his parish had an unusual number of visitors, as pilgrims even then came from all over to see the holy places.

Now there is rather less of a stable continuing community, and the people thronging the church's sacred precincts consist overwhelmingly of visitors, most of whom will never return. Thus, there is no baptistery—that sign of a stable and growing community—found in the present church, for it is not so much a community as a place of pilgrimage.

In the days of Egeria, all the faithful worshipped together as a body at the main altar in the Martyrium. Now there are a number of small chapels with their altars, each of which serves a different group of visitors. Yet one thing remains, a constant stretching from the first days of the apostles to the present, through all the changes and chances that have bombarded and afflicted that church: the presence of Golgotha and the empty tomb. That site, those few sacred meters, was the historical magnet that drew lovers of Christ from all over. In the days of Egeria, it was the heart of parish life for the local Christians of Aelia. Even now it abides in Christianity as a witness to God's power and love, and issues its wordless call to all Christians to come and fall down and worship before Christ our God.

The Site of the Last Supper
The Syrian Church of St. Mark and the Cenacle

> *In the church called "Holy Zion" is the throne of James, the Lord's brother, who is buried near the Temple. It has been built in the place where after His Passion the Lord appeared to the disciples as they were at supper, "the doors being shut."*
>
> EGERIA, DESCRIBING THE SITE
> OF THE LAST SUPPER

During our first day in the Holy City we also visited the Syrian Church of St. Mark. Despite the English part of its church sign designating it as "Syrian," it has no connection with the Antiochian Orthodox Church in Syria with which the Church of the Holy Sepulcher is in communion; perhaps "Syriac" would be a better translation of its name. This church is one of the non-Chalcedonian churches (the so-called Monophysite group).

According to one source, this church has only about 2000 members in Israel, with 500 in Jerusalem and another 1500 in Bethlehem.

The church advertises itself in a sign printed in Arabic and English as "The Upper Room, the House of St. Mark, the first church in Christianity." That is, it claims to be the site of the upper room where Christ celebrated the Last Supper with His disciples and where they later made their headquarters, the so-called Zion of later church history. If so, this place (now a convent) is indeed the oldest Christian site in the world. But I wondered if it were in fact so.

A few of its other claims also raised my eyebrows a little, such as its claim to have the font in which the Virgin Mary was baptized, its claim to have an icon of the Virgin Mary and her Child painted by St. Luke, and its claim that the much-decorated door to the church was the very one knocked on by St. Peter in Acts 12:13. The church is indeed built over a grotto (as many of the buildings in Jerusalem seem to be), and the building was evidently of Crusader construction, built in turn over Byzantine ruins. Steps descending to the grotto below led to a small chapel with the usual altar and late iconography. But its claim to be the church of the upper room and the original headquarters of the apostles jostles with the historic claims of another site in Jerusalem, the Cenacle (from the Latin *cenaculum*, the room where Christ and His disciples ate the Last Supper), now upstairs on the site of the so-called Tomb of David.

In the fourth century, the Christians of Jerusalem called the original house-church and apostolic headquarters Zion, and it was described as "small" by St. Epiphanius of Cyprus, who had lived in Palestine for twenty years in the fourth century. Like many church properties in Jerusalem, it was probably destroyed by Diocletian in about 303. Later in that century, after Constantine began to favor the Christians, it was rebuilt on a larger scale. The Christians of Jerusalem in the fourth century believed this was the original apostolic meeting place. It shows up on the famous sixth-century Madaba mosaic map of the Holy Land (now in Jordan), which indicates that the new Zion church was of considerable size.

It appears this Zion church was located just beyond the city walls at their southwest corner. Near this site today we not only find the so-called Tomb of David, but also the Church of the Dormition. It would seem the site of the original Byzantine church that was built on these grounds is now covered by both the Dormition church and the Tomb of David, and that the Cenacle connection with the whole site is an echo of the original house of Mary the mother of John Mark, where the Last Supper was held.

Indeed, it could be that the connection with the Virgin Mary, whose death, or dormition, is commemorated in the nearby church, is due to a medieval confusion of Mary the mother of John Mark with Mary the Mother of God. Obviously there is no way to be certain one way or the other. But I could more easily believe that the Byzantines were basing the location of their new church on real surviving memories of the true site of the Last Supper than that the claims of the Cenacle are groundless. It seems to me that the small and struggling Syriac church of St. Mark is doing its best to shore up support by making competing claims for one of the churches they occupy in the Old City.

I can well understand the attraction of thinking the Syriac church was the original site of the Last Supper. In its rival site with the better claim, the Cenacle upstairs from the so-called Tomb of David, nothing remains that would excite Christian piety. We wandered about in its rooms, looking for echoes of a holy past, but found nothing left on which devotion could fasten, nothing to suggest the sacred meal, or the apostolic headquarters, or the Byzantine church St. Cyril of Jerusalem described as "the upper church of the apostles" and in which Egeria later worshipped.

The present Cenacle was built by the Crusaders in the fourteenth century, and one cannot pinpoint there the actual place where Christ reclined with His disciples at the Supper. Instead, the whole site bears the marks of its past use by Muslims and its present use by Orthodox Jews. I looked in vain for hints of where the Supper might have been eaten, or even for fleeting shadows of my beloved Egeria. I left the place feeling empty, and my heart felt cold, even in the hot Palestinian sun. The most I could gather from my visit was the thought that somewhere near here, perhaps within five hundred yards from where I was wandering, the original gathering place of the apostolic church once stood. Never had Egeria felt so far away or the Christian past so deeply buried.

For many pilgrims, such considerations and uncertainty are too much for their piety to bear. Piety wants to touch the actual spot where sacred events occurred—to stand in a certain place and know that here, *right here*, on the spot where I am standing right now, Christ held the Last Supper. Or that *there*, on that very patch of ground, He knelt in the Garden of Gethsemane and sweated blood in prayer. Or that right over *there* was the place where He broke bread with the disciples on the shore of the Sea of Tiberias after the Resurrection. Such intense desire to find the exact spot finds it all but intolerable to be told these events occurred not exactly *here*, but somewhere in this approximate area. Worse yet to such pious desire are the pronouncements of scholars that offer degrees of certitude: "It is probable that the Last Supper was held on this site, but there is a slim possibility that it was held on the rival site."

The fact is that absolute certainty is not possible about everything, so informed piety is forced to use a sliding scale of probable authenticity. The authenticity of some sites is all but certain: the hill of Golgotha, the Lord's Tomb, the well at Nazareth. A number of factors contribute to the case for certainty: the antiquity of the site's claims, the continuity of devotion at the site, and the nature of the site itself (in the case of Mary's well in Nazareth, for example, there was only one well in that small hamlet in Christ's day, and wells do not move). Other sites command less certainty, but still have a degree of probability: sites like the location of Pilate's praetorium or the place of the Last Supper. Other sites have even less probability and are almost certainly spurious, such as the place on the wall along the Via Dolorosa where Christ leaned on the way to Golgotha, leaving the imprint of His hand.

Such varying degrees of certainty can actually aid our faith and maturity. Admittedly our desire to connect with the sacred past pushes us to find the exact spots where these events happened. We long to kiss a given square foot of sacred earth and know that our lips are venerating the authentic place to which our mind directs. It interferes with the emotional act of veneration to think, "Maybe I am kissing ground on which He never trod—ordinary earth—and the sacred spot I intend to kiss is somewhere over there." Piety cannot easily feed on such doubts and calculations. Easier to believe the guides and tell oneself that, no, on this very square foot of earth where I am standing right now (or which I am photographing) the Lord celebrated the Supper, or prayed in Gethsemane.

Piety cannot feed on scholarship. But the cautions of scholarship can still serve to remind the pious that our hope lies not in the accuracy of our pious pilgrimage, but in our faith in God and in His mercy. It reminds us that we are saved, not by ascertaining the authentic and accurate route of the Via Dolorosa, but by trusting in Christ, who trod that way for us, by whatever route.

The sacred events are saving because they are apprehended by faith, not because they are recovered by physical presence at the spots where they occurred. Perhaps this is all Gregory of Nyssa meant to convey by his negative assessment of pilgrimage. One can find salvation and grow in holiness even if one never venerates the actual holy places, or even if one never sets foot in the Holy Land at all.

~: 3 :~

The Mount of Olives

Walking Through the Old City

Before our visit to the *Mount of Olives*, my traveling companion and I returned once again to the Old City (as we would many times during our trip, the Orthodox iron within us responding to the magnetic pull of the Church of the Holy Sepulcher). As well as praying again and again in that holy place, we had other tasks to perform, such as purchasing gifts for family, loved ones, and others in our church back home. (We also had to eat. A piece of pilgrim advice: Never sit down in a *suq*, or shop, to eat before asking, "How much?")

So it was that we wandered through the narrow and tangled streets of the Old City many times, both of us wearing our customary cassocks. As an Orthodox priest, I of course also wore my pectoral cross, the usual attire for priests. I was somewhat unprepared for what happened to me repeatedly whenever we walked through those winding lanes. For about a dozen times in three days, I was spat at.

Well, not me, precisely, but rather my pectoral cross. I didn't notice the first time it happened, since I had my gaze firmly focused on the uneven cobblestones beneath me. I am effectively blind in one eye and so have no real depth perception, and the streets present me with a challenge if I am to avoid constantly tripping. Hence the downward gaze. But there was nothing wrong with my deacon's eyes, and he instantly noticed.

"Did you see that man spitting at you?" he asked.

The man in question was an ultra-Orthodox Jew, with the usual black coat, black hat, white shirt, and swinging earlocks. He was accompanied by his young son, identically attired. They were out walking through the streets of the Old City, doubtless on the way to or from some errand. As he passed, he audibly spat at my cross. In the next few days, the action was repeated again and again by other ultra-Orthodox Jews, and sometimes by the little boys in company with their fathers. I was not particularly traumatized. I only mentioned to my friend that the one spitting was probably not working for the Israeli Department of Tourism.

Afterward I did some research on such behavior, and found that this was not unusual in the Old City. Indeed, the June 6, 2013, headline of the Jewish newspaper *HaAretz* read,

"Ultra-Orthodox spitting attacks on Old City clergymen becoming daily."

It should be noted that many Israelis do not condone such behavior and even strenuously condemn it. One judge, Dov Pollock, wrote in a legal opinion that "suffering the degradation of being spat on while walking around in church robes [was] a fundamental contravention of the principles of justice and decency." One Jewish government minister, Avraham Poraz, condemned the trend of spitting at the cross and those wearing it, saying it was "intolerable" and that he was "revolted" by it.

It is thus unfair to ascribe what is customary among the ultra-Orthodox to Jews everywhere. But it is still the normal experience of Christian clergy in the Old City (especially, apparently, the Armenian clergy), and such things do nothing to cool the spiritual temperature there, which in many ways stands in great need of cooling.

What causes this, I wondered? What would cause one stranger to spit at another, in the complete absence of personal provocation? In a word: tribalism, the balkanization of the human race which divides a man from his brothers, so that he sees before him not a person but a member of the Enemy, of the warring tribe. When this tribalism seizes and possesses the human heart, one's neighbor (defined biblically as the person standing in front of one) is stripped of multidimensionality. He becomes rather a creature of one dimension, having neither name, nor history, nor personal virtues, nor sorrows.

We see this throughout our tragic history. I remember a BBC interview of a man who had committed atrocities against the Jews of his town during the Second World War, shooting men, women, and children. When the interviewer asked (with some heat), "Why in God's name would you shoot a child who has no political views and who is no danger to you?" he simply replied, "They were Jews." That is, for this man, the people cowering before him were not really persons. For him they had no names and were utterly unlike him. They had no joys or sorrows, no fears or aspirations. They were faceless, phantoms, members of the Other, the Enemy, regardless of their age or gender. Jews. Shooting them therefore had no moral significance. The man did not feel guilty. He did not feel pleased. He did not feel anything. Regarding those before him as mere phantoms, he had become a phantom himself.

We see this tribalism today working in the minds of Islamic terrorists. For those planting and exploding bombs, the people harmed and killed are scarcely persons. They are the Enemy, a threat to Islam, a dark and dangerous part of the *Dar al-Harb*. My tribe wars against yours, and individuals have no reality apart from being members of the enemy tribe.

It is an old story, and the forces of tribalism are invoked by leaders every time men go to war. The opposing side must be stripped of humanity, and the first step in this demonic process is a linguistic one. The German foe is no longer a German, but a Kraut; the Vietnamese enemy soldier is no longer a Vietnamese, but a Gook. Such artifices are necessary if a decent man is to be persuaded to kill a complete stranger. When such tribalism begins to give way, it is harder to wage war.

Witness the famous Christmas Eve truce in the First World War. The men sitting close to each other in their own trenches, a few scant yards across No Man's Land, began to converse and (significantly) to sing Christmas carols. Soon they emerged and met in No Man's Land, and began talking more. They showed each other photos of loved ones, and exchanged news and personal tokens. They ate and drank together. They played a game of football (soccer). This was quite alarming to the leaders, who solemnly and vociferously condemned such camaraderie across "enemy lines." And with reason, for now to each soldier the person sitting armed in the opposing trench was not the Enemy, but a person, someone not unlike himself. Having seen photos of the enemy's wife and children back home, it was harder to shoot him and make that woman a widow and her children fatherless. A member of the enemy tribe had become a neighbor.

Such a process of eroding tribalism is, I believe, the only hope for peace in the cauldron that is the Old City and the State of Israel. The temptation, when spat upon by an ultra-Orthodox Jew, is to spit back—or at least to classify ultra-Orthodox Jews as the Enemy, the Intolerant Ones, Those Who Spit. Hope can be found only in the Gospel and in following the precepts of Christ. When Christ counseled His disciples to turn the other cheek when hit and insulted, He did more than simply break the endless and vicious cycle of mutual hitting. He allowed us to see the hitter as our neighbor, as someone with a name, with sorrows, with many dimensions.

Such Gospel nonretaliation is not simple passivity, nor is it weakness. Rather it taps into the strength of God, who loves all His children, and it is therefore the strongest thing in the world. And it is the only thing strong enough to open eyes blind to the humanity of the Other and to exorcise the demons of tribalism.

Gethsemane

When the cock begins to crow everyone leaves the Imbomon [on the Mount of Olives] and comes down with singing to the places where the Lord prayed. The bishop and all the people go into a graceful church which has been built there and have a prayer appropriate to the place and the day, and one suitable hymn. From there all of them, including the smallest children, now go down with singing and conduct the bishop to Gethsemane. So that all can see, they are provided with hundreds of church candles. When everyone arrives at Gethsemane, they have a prayer and then a reading from the Gospel about the Lord's arrest. By the time it has been read everyone is

The Mount of Olives

> *groaning and lamenting, weeping so loud that people even across in the city can probably hear it all.*
>
> EGERIA, CHAPTER 36, DESCRIBING THE SERVICES IN GETHSEMANE

One of our visits on the Mount of Olives was to the Garden of Gethsemane. As I stood looking at the vista and the distance from the Old City walls to that garden, I was struck by the fact that in all my years of reading the New Testament, I seemed to have gotten my distances wrong. A phrase like "when Jesus had spoken these words, He went forth with His disciples across the Brook Kidron, where there was a garden" (John 18:1) flows quickly off the tongue, but I had not realized how deep and far that valley was. Looking at the vista from a height, the distance was not far as the crow flies, but it was far enough for a man to walk, especially late at night, when our Lord and His disciples walked from the place of their Jerusalem supper to the enclosed solitude of the garden.

It would appear that our Lord had connections with the people who owned the olive grove. They seem to have put it at His disposal as a place of solitude and prayer while He was in Jerusalem, which is how Judas knew that He would retire there after the Passover meal with His disciples, since this was His custom while there (Luke 22:39), and since He "often met there with His disciples" (John 18:2).

In our Lord's day the garden grove was larger than it

presently is and rather more wild—the Franciscans have made it into a happy garden with flowers. (The Franciscan passion for taming a site is well known; one writer once suggested that if given their way, the Franciscans would drain the Sea of Galilee, build a church over it, and place there a sign which read, "This is where the Sea of Galilee used to be.")

I was actually somewhat disappointed at my first sight of the garden. From my lifelong reading of the Gospels, I was ready to find the grove somewhat wilder and untamed, with olive trees growing more or less haphazardly and naturally. The neat garden patches and the smallness of the grove came as a shock to my expectations and jarred my devotional sense. And one who has been taught that Christ prayed somewhere out in the open here, by the trees, can't help asking the fatal question, "I wonder which tree was it?" No use to ask that question: the trees, of course, could not be the original trees, for history records that the Romans cut down all the trees in the area when they besieged Jerusalem in AD 70. The trees there now are very old (one has been carbon dated to 1092), but they cannot be the original ones. And there is also a possibility that Christ did not in fact encamp with His disciples out in the open under the trees at all (despite the patch of rock by the main altar in the Roman Catholic Church of All Nations purporting to be the actual patch of ground on which our Lord prayed), but in the cave or grotto nearby.

This view calls attention to the fact that the Synoptic

Gospels do not actually say Christ entered into "the *garden* of Gethsemane" but rather "to a *place* called Gethsemane" (Matt. 26:36; Mark 14:32, emphasis added). The Greek word here translated "place" is *chorion*, indicating a property. John's Gospel describes the locale as a *kepos*, a cultivated tract of land. Given the fact that there was a large cave on this *kepos* and that the word *Gethsemane* derives from the Hebrew *gat shemanim*, "press for oils," it seems likely that the cave held the oil presses.

A long tradition maintains that Christ's disciples slept here, and a chapel was built in the grotto in the fourth century. The cave is certainly large enough to have contained all of them and to allow Christ to depart from them for "a stone's throw" (Luke 22:41, Gr. *lithou bolen*), for the cave measured about thirty-six by sixty feet, over two thousand square feet. When Judas came with his armed contingent to arrest Christ, John 18:4 says that Christ "went out" (Gr. *exelthen*) to meet them. The question then is: From what did Christ go out? Not from the *kepos* or garden itself, for a witness of the arrest later asks Peter, "Did I not see you in the *kepos*?" (John 18:26). Most likely, then, Christ went out of the cave in which He was praying and in which His disciples were sleeping. This makes more sense than them sleeping out in the open on such a cold night (later that night Peter and others would be happy to stand and warm themselves by a fire; John 18:18. Why sleep in the open when a cave was nearby?

It seems to me that the view with the most to commend it is the one that places the Lord's agonized prayer, the disciples' sleep, and the final arrest at the cave, not among the olive trees beside the church, nor within the spot prepared within the church itself. This is also consistent with the statement of Egeria in her travelogue that those entering Gethsemane were provided with candles so they could see (ch. 36). This fits better with the view that Egeria and her fellow pilgrims were entering a place that was darker than outside—that is, in a cave. This is confirmed by an early sixth-century account that calls Gethsemane "a cave" (Theodosius's *De Situ Terrae Sanctae*, ch. 10).

Regardless of the actual spot at which Christ prayed, the Franciscan site provides a valuable geographical marker and a prayerful place for reflection. Somewhere nearby, Christ knelt in agony and aligned His will with the Father's. In the resolution of that agony, we find our own peace.

The Tomb of The Mother of God

Gethsemane is also said to contain another treasure, namely the tomb of the Mother of God. It is now reached by descending about fifty steps, but in New Testament times the tomb would have been located on ground level. Excavations were done in 1972 by a Franciscan archeologist Bellarmino Bagatti, who found evidence of a cemetery that he dated to the first century. He concluded that the cemetery consisted of three chambers, the actual tomb being the inner chamber of the whole complex. Early Christians believed this was the tomb of the Lord's

Mother. It was isolated from the other tombs by cutting away the surrounding rock face, and a small edicule was built over the tomb. The church over it was built in the fifth century but destroyed by the Persians in their invasion of 614. The crypt, however, was not harmed.

The story of the death of the Mother of God exists in many versions. Some traditions maintain she accompanied St. John to Ephesus and died there. Some traditions contend that she died in Palestine and was buried in Gethsemane. This latter tradition is surely more likely, for it is supremely unlikely that John would have taken an aging Jewish widow with him to a town as large, bustling, and pagan as Ephesus. It is far more likely that the Lord's command to him to care for His Mother (John 19:27) meant that John stayed in Jerusalem and kept her safely in his care there, supported by the local church (see Acts 1:14). This is further confirmed by the early presence of the Byzantine church built over the site of her reputed tomb in the fifth century and also by the many versions of the story of her passing, usually called the *Transitus Mariae*.

In the Greek version of the story, "the apostles carried the bed and laid her precious and holy body in Gethsemane in a new tomb. And behold, an odor of sweet savor came out of the holy sepulcher of our Lady the Mother of God, and until three days were past the voices of invisible angels were heard glorifying Christ our God who was born of her. And when the third day was fulfilled the voices were heard no more, and thereafter we all perceived that her spotless and precious body was translated into Paradise."

In the Latin version ascribed to Melito, Christ appears to the apostles as they are burying her, raises her from the dead, and brings her up with Him on a cloud in glory to Paradise. In yet another version, the apostles bury the body in "the valley of Jehoshaphat." Then a heavenly light shines around them so that they fall to the earth, and angels take up the body to heaven, unseen by the apostles. Thomas, however, saw the ascending body from a distance, for he was being brought miraculously to the Mount of Olives while serving the Liturgy in his church in India, still wearing his eucharistic vestments. The other apostles, who did not see her taken up as Thomas did, chided him for being late and told him that she was buried in her tomb. Thomas (who this time had it over the others; compare John 20:24–29) insisted they were wrong and that her body was not there, but that she had been taken to heaven. When they all went to her tomb to show her body to Thomas, they indeed discovered she was gone.

The one constant in all the stories is her burial in Gethsemane, near the valley of Jehoshaphat (that is, the Kidron Valley)—as well as, of course, her being received bodily into Paradise after her death. The Greek version of the story, though naturally not devoid of miracles (the literary genre of the *Transitus* required many miracles), is the most restrained regarding her actual translation to heaven.

In transposing one genre into another and looking at the miracle-studded story to find the authentically historical kernel within it, we may arrive at the following. It seems Mary died in Jerusalem while in the care of John and was buried by the local church of Jerusalem in the tomb on the Gethsemane property. I suggest that her body was translated to heaven unseen by any, and that the church became aware of it when pilgrims came to venerate her body and found it gone. But whatever elements of the miraculous one accepts in the story of her passing, the claim of the Tomb of Mary in Gethsemane to represent the original site of her burial would seem to be well founded.

My companion and I descended a long series of forty-seven steps to enter the grotto, which was on ground level in the first century. The iconography revealed that it was under the care of the Greek Orthodox, who share the site with Christians of other confessions. This gave it all a fairly cluttered look, which made my devotion a bit more difficult. We entered the edicule that had been built over her tomb and saw the tomb of Mary itself. The bare rock that once held her dead body had been encased in marble and glass, over which hung many candles and icons.

I closed my eyes and tried to visualize the tomb in the first century, my imagination willing away the gorgeous edicule encrusted with icons and the innumerable silver hanging lamps suspended from the ceiling like Byzantine stalactites. Centuries of devoted love had made this crowded shrine, but I would've given anything for just one moment to see it all gone and to stand in the original unadorned tomb.

When the Mother of God was first laid there, it was a rough and terrible place, as all tombs were—a cold, lonely place where death and darkness and decay claimed all. The mourners of the Jerusalem church laid her to rest with tears, numb with love and sorrow, little thinking her Son would soon rescue His Mother from the stench of corruption. I longed to open my eyes and see only the rough stone sepulcher and its cold severity, a fitting contrast to the glory of Christ that would later fill the tomb and raise the Mother of God to new life. Instead, I opened my eyes and saw the gold and silver riza on the icon of the Dormition above the tomb. I looked once more at the bare rock behind the glass and walked back up the steps to the light of the twenty-first century.

The Chapel of The Ascension

All the people go home for a rest, and as soon as they have had their meal, they go up Eleona, the Mount of Olives, each at his own pace, till there is not a Christian left in the city. Once they have climbed Eleona, the Mount of Olives, they go to the Imbomon (the place from which the Lord ascended into heaven), where the bishop takes his seat, and also the presbyters and all the people. They have readings and prayers and the gospel

The Mount of Olives

> *reading about the Lord's ascension. At three o'clock they go down with singing from there to the other church on Eleona, containing the cave where the Lord used to sit and teach the apostles.*
>
> EGERIA, CHAPTER 43, DESCRIBING THE SERVICES ON THE MOUNT OF OLIVES FOR THE ASCENSION

That afternoon on the Mount of Olives we also visited the site marking the Ascension of Christ. In the days of Egeria, this was not a church, but a circular colonnaded rotunda built on the summit of the Mount of Olives, for she writes in her famous travelogue not that there was a church there, but that here one could sit down. It was called the Imbomen, from the Greek *en bouno*, "on the hillock." Later a lady named Poemenia, a member of the imperial family, enlarged the site into an actual church. This structure was destroyed by the Persians when they invaded in 614. It was rebuilt later that same century only to be, later still, destroyed by the Muslims.

All that is left of the structure is a small chapel, about three meters square, standing in the midst of the original Byzantine church ruins. Originally, like the Imbomen Egeria knew, this structure was open to the sky, but its Muslim owners roofed it over and bricked up the spaces between the columns. It remains in Muslim hands, and they charge a small fee for Christians to enter the site.

The present chapel is not very impressive, as the current Muslim owners have not taken pains to adorn what is essentially now a Christian site. Christian services are allowed in the area, but only outside the chapel, in the courtyard around it. Though the chapel does mark the authentic site where Christians have commemorated the Ascension of Christ since the fourth century, it does not mark the site of the actual Ascension itself. In Luke 24:50, we read that Christ led His disciples out "as far as Bethany" and ascended from there—in other words, over the summit of the Mount of Olives and down the other side toward Bethany. But it is hard to build a chapel on a hillside, and we can scarcely blame the Byzantines for building their chapel on the more obvious spot on the hillock's summit. (This means, of course, that the stone within the Imbomen chapel said by guides to be the very place from which Christ ascended and upon which He left His footprint cannot be authentic.)

I walked around inside the chapel and stared upward at the interior of its now-covered-over roof. And the longer I stared, the more I thought this roofing over of the Imbomen was something more than a bit of cloddish architectural insensitivity. I came to think it represented a difference between the spiritualities of the two rival communities, between the Christians who built it, leaving it open to the sky, and the Muslims who roofed it over.

The Christians who first built the Imbomen, whether the more minimal rotunda Egeria knew or the larger church built later that century, certainly knew how to roof over their buildings, and most of their churches of course had roofs. But this one they deliberately left open to the sky, inviting the worshippers within to look up. That was significant, because the Ascension of Christ from earth to heaven and His glorification constitutes a promise and pledge that we also will one day share that ascended glory.

Christian theology insists that salvation consists of sharing Christ's glory (Rom. 8:29–30; 1 John 3:2). The fancy name for this process is *theosis*, divinization, and it means that what Christ is by nature, He shares with us by grace, God becoming man so that man could become divine. That is why the Ascension of Christ is not just an event in His own history, but also a pledge of what will, by grace, become our history as well. And that is why the original Christians looked up to the sky while worshipping in the Imbomen, to imagine their Lord ascending into heaven and to look forward to the day when they would follow Him home.

Islamic theology of course holds a different view of salvation, one in which divinization is not merely excluded from our destiny but actually considered to be a blasphemous idea. Muslims accept that Jesus ascended into heaven (though they deny that He died on the cross and that He rose from the dead afterward), but they roofed over the shrine commemorating this event nonetheless. For them, man cannot become divine. It is no good looking up at what will never be; better to look to Mecca.

I enjoyed entering the chapel of the Ascension and looking up to its roof. I enjoyed even more coming out of that place and looking up with freedom into heaven. For the Christian, the sky is literally the limit.

There was not much to see in the chapel except the inauthentic "footprint" of Christ and the roof Islamic heresy had built—nothing to ignite the flame of devotion. This was, I suppose, deliberate and the whole point of the Muslims not allowing the Christians to transform the chapel into a place of Christian prayer or to hold services within it. But as I walked about in the enclosed Imbomen, Egeria came to my rescue. She had seen this place and sat here, listened to the Gospel readings intoned by the local clergy, and offered her prayers to the ascended God. My steps intersected with hers, though separated by centuries. She had prayed there at a happier time, amidst a joyful throng of exultant believers. I could only stroll about a cold place where she had once walked, and remember, and lament a past long lost.

The Church of the Pater Noster

On the Mount of Olives, we also found and visited the Church of the Pater Noster, now (as the Latin title indicates) in Roman Catholic hands. It is so called because of the multitude of placards placed throughout the church, each one giving the text of the Lord's Prayer (in Latin the *Pater noster*, "our Father") in a different language. It was very nice, but it was not the reason

The Mount of Olives

I was anxious to visit this site. I wanted badly to see this place because it was built over the site of the original Eleona church, the Byzantine church on the Mount of Olives (*eleona* is from the Greek for "olive grove"), the church in which Egeria worshipped, and the place in which they commemorated the Ascension before the church of the Imbomen was built. The Eleona church was built over the cave on the Mount of Olives where Christ sat to teach His disciples Peter, James, John, and Andrew about the destruction of Jerusalem and the end of the world (Mark 13:3).

Not unexpectedly, little remains of these original sites. One can see bits of the original cave and some walls of the Eleona church still standing outside the Church of the Pater Noster. I found my way down to the cave, closed my eyes, and imagined that if I turned my head quickly enough I might see Peter and James and John and Andrew sitting somewhere nearby, listening to Christ. And I thought of Egeria, sitting in the large and spacious beauty of the Eleona church and listening to the clergy read those words of Christ three centuries later.

The ruins of the Eleona, both its cave below and its Byzantine remains above, witness to the relentless stream of history in which all Christian life is lived. The large and splendid church that Constantine built and in which Egeria worshipped is long gone, its few remaining walls standing like sad sentinels to give their forlorn and mute witness to an earlier glory. The tourists scarcely give those walls and that glory a thought; they are more interested in the present church, which offers its placards with the Lord's Prayer in a multitude of languages, most of which were unknown in the time of Christ. I hurried through the modern church and hardly gave it a look. I already knew the words of the Lord's Prayer. My heart looked for the apostles, and for the Eleona, and for Egeria.

The ruins of the Eleona church witness to the layered life that is the Holy Land. Archeologists know this quite well—how one generation dies and succeeding generations build on top of them, with layer piled on layer. Given how long the Holy Land has known continuing devastation and rebuilding (the inevitable cost of being located on the land bridge between Africa and Asia, so that every army that ever marched tromped through their backyard and conquered them on the way to someplace else), it is not surprising to find such layers. Digging deepest brings one to the Canaanite layer, overtop of which is the Israelite layer. Then comes the Hasmonean layer and then the Herodian. Then the Roman layer, the Byzantine one, the Muslim one, the Crusader one, and the Ottoman one. And now the modern Palestinian and Israeli one. The entire Holy Land could be considered one vast archeological dig.

Pilgrims naturally want to go there and find things as they were in the days of Christ, with Bethlehem and Nazareth being small, quiet hamlets, and a few shepherds knocking about with their sheep. They want to see an unspoiled Garden of Gethsemane, with its olive trees two thousand years old. They want to enter the Old City and see the "green hill, far away" that they have been singing about all their lives, and to find an unspoiled Garden Tomb. If they are a certain kind of Protestant, their Protestantism bids them jump over church history into the Land of the Bible and find in Palestine the pristine Bible of their reading and their imagination.

It is jarring and disconcerting to find that history did not stop with the death of the last apostle and that Christians have continued to live in the Holy Land and build there for the last two thousand years. It is an offense to pious imagination to enter the Church of the Holy Sepulcher and find Byzantium; it is traumatic to drive to Nazareth and find a modern city with stores, advertising, and traffic jams, rather than a pastoral rural hamlet of five hundred people with women drawing water from its single well.

Certainly there is no shortage of guides in the Holy Land who will oblige the tourist's desire to ignore the necessities of history and who will happily point out signs of the Lord's activity lying right on the surface, pointing to this handprint or that footprint that Christ made two millennia ago, guides who will point to that container there as the one that held the water Christ turned to wine. But authentic historical memorials are not so easily recovered. Layer has succeeded layer, and today's pilgrim must burrow through the past to find the Land of the Bible.

This is true also of the Mount of Olives. The cave in which our Lord sat when He taught His disciples is buried beneath the Eleona church, and this is buried in the past also. The pilgrim who seeks to find Christ's presence on the Mount of Olives must dig down, think back, and realize that the river of time flows ever on.

Indeed, the whole Mount of Olives witnesses to such change. In Gethsemane the Lord passed His last hours of solitude and prayer, preparing Himself inwardly for the final hours of His life. At the tomb of the Mother of God nearby, His Mother's final remains were reverently laid to rest, and it was here that she stepped from time into eternity. On the summit of the Mount of Olives the Lord's Ascension is marked, where He spoke His last words to the apostles and then broke the bonds of time and space to sit at the Father's right hand. On the Mount of Olives we find the cave in which Christ sat with a few of His disciples and prepared them for the end of Jerusalem, when it would perish in chaos and flame; and there we find also the beautiful Byzantine Eleona church built over it, which at length suffered the same fate as Jerusalem.

All of Olivet seems to reverberate with echoes of the end that eventually overtakes all mortal flesh. To stand on Olivet is to be surrounded by the monuments and memorials of mortality. It is a beautiful place, but the wind blowing through its olive trees sings a sad song, telling us that all must die, and be buried, and step from time into eternity. It bids us give thought now to what we will find when we take that final step.

~: 4 :~

Bethlehem
and Judea

The Church of the Nativity, Bethlehem

The fortieth day after Pascha is a Thursday. On the previous day, Wednesday, everyone goes in the afternoon for the vigil service to Bethlehem, where it is held in the church containing the cave where the Lord was born.

EGERIA, CHAPTER 43, REFERRING
TO THE CHURCH IN BETHLEHEM

If Jerusalem is the hope of the Christian, Bethlehem is his childhood. This is especially true of children of the West such as myself, who grew up singing Christmas carols and returned each year in spirit to the little town of Bethlehem before I could even find it on a world map. My earliest imaginations were nurtured by images of the Holy Family in the stable, Mary and Joseph bending low over the Christ Child with ox and ass waiting beside them like acolytes at an altar, and with shepherds and Wise Men (three of them, kings) drawing near. It was always snowing, but never cold.

It was also, I might have added had I known, always in northern Europe. Christmas is usually cold in northern Europe, and often with obliging snowfall on Christmas Eve. In my childish world, I was living in a kind of Currier and Ives Christmas card. All of this can make the first visit to the shrine of the Nativity in Bethlehem a bit difficult for us Western Christians from up north, as deep-seated assumptions and long-cherished images clash with authentic history and the present ecclesiastical reality.

Most of the images from my childhood Christmas were not drawn from the Gospel. Luke simply relates that Joseph went down to his ancestral Bethlehem during the time of the required census, accompanied by his (very) pregnant wife Mary, and "while they were there, the days were completed for her to be delivered. And she brought forth her firstborn Son, and wrapped Him in swaddling cloths, and laid Him in a manger, because there was no room for them in the inn" (Luke 2:6–7). Shepherds, informed of the birth by angels, came to see the newborn Child and "found Mary and Joseph, and the Babe lying in a manger" (v. 16).

Note that the ox and ass, which "before Him bowed" in the Christmas carols, are nowhere in sight. In fact they appear in our Nativity imagery not from St. Luke's sober narrative, but courtesy of Christian preaching on the prophecies of Isaiah. When the prophet lamented concerning disobedient Israel, "The ox knows its owner / And the donkey its master's crib; / But Israel does not know, / My people do not consider" (Is. 1:3), Christian preachers saw in the lament a prophecy of the birth of Christ in the manger. Thereafter the animals' place in the Christmas crèche was assured. But there is nothing in the Gospel text to suggest that the cave and its manger were in use when the Holy Family commandeered the place.

Bethlehem in the first century was a tiny hamlet, so small that it scarcely showed up in the demographics. Even in the old days before the Babylonian exile it was pretty small, and the prophet Micah (who lived in the seventh century BC), acknowledges this when he speaks of the little hamlet. The future king, the descendant of David, would arise from David's hometown of Bethlehem, and yet the prophet still describes the town with the words, "you, Bethlehem Ephrathah, / Though you are little among the thousands of Judah" (Micah 5:2). The Greek Septuagint of the text preserves this admission of the tininess of the town.

It is only in St. Matthew's citation of the prophetic text that the town's outward size comes to reflect its inward greatness: "You, Bethlehem, *in* the land of Judah, are not the least among the rulers of Judah" (Matt. 2:6). Matthew of course is not translating; he is making a point, as all good Jewish interpreters did. But we must not miss the historical fact that Bethlehem in the Lord's day did not really show up on anyone's demographic radar. That was probably why Josephus did not bother to mention the slaughter of the innocents there by Herod soon after the birth of Christ. What was the death of a few babies and toddlers in a nothing place like Bethlehem compared to all the other crimes of Herod?

It seems clear enough that it would not take much to fill up the town and that if a number of people like Joseph arrived there, it would be hard for them to find lodging with anyone, either at the khan (the usual inn for sojourners) or even boarding room with families and friends. Thus the Holy Family was forced to find shelter in a cave. Northern Europeans, reading about a manger, assumed that the manger must have been located in an outbuilding like the stables they knew back home. But that it was a cave and not an outbuilding is confirmed by the persistence and antiquity of traditions referring to a cave.

St. Justin Martyr, writing in the second century, says, "Joseph took up his quarters in a certain cave near the village, and while they were there Mary brought forth the Christ and placed Him in a manger" (*Dial. with Trypho*, ch. 78). The apocryphal *Protoevangelium of James*, written about the same time, narrates the birth of Christ with a wealth of miracles and assumes the locale was a cave: Joseph "found a cave there, and led [Mary] into it."

Origen, in his work *Against Celsus*, writes in 248, "In Bethlehem the cave is pointed out where He was born, and the manger in the cave where He was wrapped in swaddling clothes. And the rumor is in those places, and among foreigners of the Faith, that indeed Jesus was born in this cave who is worshipped and reverenced by the Christians" (1.51).

Jerome, writing in 395 from the very site about his "own beloved Bethlehem" speaks of "the very cave where the infant Christ had uttered His earliest cry" (*Ep. 58, to Paulinus*). There is therefore no reason to doubt the reliability of such a persistent and early tradition.

Here, however, one needs to deal with a comparatively recent rethinking of the situation of the birth of Jesus. Some scholars deny that the cave was isolated or that the Holy Family was more or less alone at the time of the birth. They point to the fact that Joseph probably had some kin remaining in Bethlehem and that these would have given them shelter. Ancient peasant homes in that day usually had a lower room or cellar where animals were housed, as well as an upper room (in Greek, a *kataluma*).

These scholars make the argument that Joseph and Mary found shelter with his extended family, and when the time came for Mary to give birth, she went down to the place where the animals were lest the birth-giving make the room or *kataluma* above ceremonially unclean (as the blood of childbirth would do). This, they say, is what Luke meant by saying, "There was no room in the inn" (Gr. *kataluma*); he was using the word *kataluma* not to indicate a khan or inn for sojourners but the upper room in a house. Admittedly this is how the word is used in Luke 22:11. So some argue that Mary gave birth to Christ in a crowded house, surrounded by supportive family.

The problem is not just that this flies in the face of our habitual imagery, but also that it is not the impression given by the Lukan narrative itself. Luke's point in saying that Mary laid Him in a manger "because there was no room for them in the *kataluma*" (Luke 2:7) functions in his overarching narrative as an image of rejection: Luke shows that Christ's rejection by His people began as soon as He was born. This loses most of its force if all Luke really meant was that Mary gave birth in the cellar because the upstairs room was already taken, but they had all the support of family there anyway.

Arguing from silence is always precarious, but the overwhelming impression given by the story is that Mary and Joseph were alone when the shepherds found them (v. 16), not that the shepherds entered a house already packed with people. The word *kataluma* can refer to the upper room of a house, but it can also refer to a khan for travelers, which is how it is used in the Septuagint Greek of Exodus 4:24. There is, I suggest, no compelling reason to abandon the traditional view that the cave was in some measure isolated from the crowds filling the small hamlet.

Either way, a large town has grown up around that small hamlet, and the place is now contained in a large city inside a bustling center of tourism. When one passes through Manger Square and enters the large Byzantine basilica that is the Church of the Nativity in Bethlehem, it takes a good imagination to see it as it must have been when Joseph first found it. Then it was in a wooded area (Jerome mentions a grove there, with the worship of the pagan Tammuz going on there before his day). Constantine eliminated the pagan worship he found there and built a large basilica over the place of the cave, finishing the work by the mid-fourth century. It was destroyed by fire during the revolts of the Samaritans in the sixth century, and later rebuilt by Justinian in 565. The original mosaic floor can be seen today through a trap door in the present flooring. By Jerome's day the original manger had been replaced by a silver one—an adornment of which Jerome did not approve. He said, "For me, the one which was removed is the more precious." Many modern pilgrims would probably agree. This place is now marked simply with a marble slab.

The present shrine, a place of marble and precious metal, all overhung with glowing lamps, makes a stunning contrast to the cave as it once was. One reaches the grotto shrine by a series of steps around the back of the altar. Like everyone else, I descended the steps and lined up to venerate the silver star that marks the place on the marble floor under the altar where Christ was born. On the star were the Latin words, "*Hic de Virgine Maria Jesus Christus Natus Est*": "Here the Virgin Mary gave birth to Jesus Christ."

When my turn came, I prostrated myself under the altar table and kissed the silver star. In that split second of prostrate veneration, I did what every other pilgrim in that place did: I closed my eyes and returned in imagination to the moment of Christ's birth two thousand years ago. Gone were the silver and the marble, gone was the Greek iconostasis groaning with icons, gone the majestic pillars of Justinian. With my closed eyes I saw only a rude, bare cave, empty save for Joseph and Mary. In this very spot, perhaps within mere yards from where I knelt, a young Mary labored with intensity and gave birth to God in the flesh. It is possible there was not even a midwife present, and that no one was present with them in that hour apart from God and prophesied destiny.

Kneeling in the grotto and walking through the nave of the church with its rows of columns gives one a sense of the grandeur of the original Byzantine structure. Some found that grandeur incongruous and felt it detracted from the miracle of the Incarnation. They would have preferred that the place had been left unspoiled and untouched by emperors so that all could better appreciate the humility the eternal Word embraced when He was born into our midst.

Yet all this decoration, so different from the images of rustic poverty portrayed on Christmas cards, cannot detract from the essential miracle that is the Incarnation. For when we stop to consider what God did, the magnitude of the divine self-emptying is not much affected by whether or not the place of birth was decorated. The pre-Incarnate Word, living and reigning with the Father and the Spirit, receiving the ceaseless adoration of seraphim and cherubim and the thunderous praises of ten thousand times ten thousand angels, became a human baby, small enough to be laid in a manger or feeding trough usually used by animals, and vulnerable enough to need warming there.

The leap from divinity to humanity, from eternity to time, from omnipotence to helplessness, from Creator to creation, is an infinite one. It beggars the imagination to attempt to understand the size of that leap or the immensity of that self-emptying. Christians have never gotten over it, and their hymnody has never ceased to celebrate it. After such a miracle, all other miracles pale by comparison. When one compares the present shrine at Bethlehem to the heavenly glory of the throne of God, Bethlehem is still a poor rustic place after all, and this rusticity should still excite our wonder. When one bows low to kiss the silver star that marks the place of Christ's birth, one pays wordless tribute to a divine condescension we will never be able to fully grasp.

As I left the church, I stopped to touch the columns of Justinian once last time, looked around, and was grateful for the house that love built.

St. Saba's Monastery

After Bethlehem, we drove east through the hot Judean desert to the site of the monastery of St. Saba, about fifteen miles from Jerusalem. The monastery is built on a steep hillside on the Kidron gorge and presents an impressive sight, since one comes upon it all at once. One moment all is barren desert and wilderness, and the next one looks at a habitation of monks who have been sanctifying that desert by their prayers for well over a thousand years. St. Saba came to this forbidding wilderness in the fifth century, and his successors have been praying there ever since.

Saba was born in Cappadocia, the child of a soldier. His parents committed him to a monastery when he was five years old, as if it were a kind of boarding school, expecting him to marry later on and lead a "normal" life. He did not. He committed himself to a life of monastic solitude when he was seventeen. At the age of thirty he went to live in a cave, abandoning the more communal monastic life he had known for this more severe experiment, while still retaining obedient connections with his original monastic community. Many monks joined him in this experiment, and eventually he took them to live in the Kidron gorge in about 484. His experiment continued to thrive, and eventually in 491 the bishop of Jerusalem ordained him a priest and gave him authority to lead all the monks in the area. St. Saba died in 532, surrounded by many hundreds of ascetics who looked to him as their father and inspiration.

Despite his political and ecclesiastical importance, Saba was primarily a cave-dweller—someone who fled from the city of man to seek the face of God in solitude. It was because he found God there that so many people joined him, imploring him to teach them how they could also find God as he had done. The mark of his success in teaching so many to follow him can be found even now in the Judean hills, for the hills are riddled with the caves of monks who lived there, following the example of Saba and finding the living God in the forbidding wilderness miles from Jerusalem.

My companion and I went to see the original cave of Saba, now made into a church. That church and the larger catholicon church built next to it that now houses his holy body witness to the greatness of his accomplishment. These buildings now, of course, look like churches, with icons and icon screens, all smelling of incense. In the days of Saba, the original church was a primitive cave, a place that echoed with his prayer and knew little beauty except the beauty of holiness. Its present splendor testifies to the splendor of Saba's soul and his quest for the living God—a splendor so palpable that thousands after him would be enchanted by it and would follow him into that desert to find it.

I looked at St. Saba's body, preserved in vestments and under glass with an aer, or cloth, covering his face, and knew that a few inches away from my gaze and touch lay the earthly remains of someone who walked with God. The catholicon that retains his relics holds a treasure beyond all counting.

His monastery, as mentioned above, has a long history. Because my companion and I wore our cassocks and were thus recognized as clergy, we were given the opportunity to view yet another treasure—the cave in which St. John of Damascus lived and worked. Almost every time we Orthodox open our liturgical books, we magnify our debt to John of Damascus, for he wrote much of our liturgical tradition. But he was not some ivory tower academic. Indeed, he did not live in a tower, but in a cave, retiring there to become a monk in about 706 after things became too difficult for Christians in Damascus.

We were blessed to descend the steps into the cave in which he prayed and slept and worked and wrote. It was a tiny space, a space that only an ascetic could have chosen and loved, a cell so small we could not stand up inside it. I sat for a brief moment on the rock on which he slept and felt an immense gratitude to him for the hymns he wrote, which enrich our Orthodox worship even today. I have never slept on a rock; I seek the comfort of a bed when I sleep. Clearly St. John did not, for he preferred the presence of God to physical comfort. The power of his poetry and hymns, used by Orthodox even to this day, vindicates the wisdom of his choice.

St. Saba's monastery stands in the desert like a sentry, keeping its watch for God throughout the centuries. Even in this cold and secular century it clings to life, refusing to die, even though its numbers are much reduced. Its monks, I thought, looked a bit as if they were under siege, which of course they are. Theirs is a thankless task, for there are few there to fulfill their monastic labors, and there are no emperors to help them now, just the occasional tourist and pilgrim. I appreciated their kindness and hospitality, but even more their courageous perseverance. We drove away from the monastery back to civilization and comfort. They stood where they had always been, alone in the desert with God.

The Jordan River

> Then I remembered that according to the Bible it was near Salim that holy John baptized at Aenon. So I asked if it was far away. "There it is," said the holy presbyter, "two hundred yards away. If you like we can walk over there." There was a kind of pool in front of the spring at which it appears holy John the Baptist exercised his ministry of baptism. A great many brothers, holy monks, from different parts, travel here to wash at this place. So once more we had a prayer and a reading at this spring, as we did in other places.
>
> EGERIA, CHAPTER 15, DESCRIBING REACHING THE JORDAN RIVER WHERE JOHN BAPTIZED

Our next stop, after visiting the dry barrens of Judean monasticism, was the Jordan River. The Jordan ranks right after Jerusalem as one of the enduring symbols of Christian piety and liturgy. At every baptism the Orthodox ask that the water in the font might be given "the blessing of Jordan," and even such nonsacramental groups as those producing what were once called Negro spirituals sang that "Jordan is chilly and cold; chills the body, but not the soul." For Christians, ever since the time when John waded into its waters and Christ sanctified its streams by His own baptism, the Jordan River is not simply a body of water, comparable to the Nile flowing through Egypt, or the Amazon flowing through South America, or the Mississippi flowing through the American South. The Jordan is the river that flows through all our lives as Christians, wherever we may chance to live.

Reflection and preaching on the Jordan started early. One Church Father noticed from reading Joshua 4:16 that the river flowed from a place called Adam up north and down to the Dead Sea in the south, and made the Jordan an image of human existence, starting from our forefather Adam and ending in death. Others have noted that the Jordan formed the geographical boundary of the Promised Land, so that Israel had to pass over the Jordan to inherit that land (see Josh. 3–4), and made the Jordan the symbol of death through which all Christians had to pass in order to enter the heavenly Promised Land. (Hence the words of the spiritual quoted above, since for the Christian death chills the body but does not touch the soul, which passes over the river of death to be with Christ.) Thus the Jordan River retains its spiritual potency for all Christians. It is not only the river in which Christ was baptized. It is also the river through which we all must pass and in which each of us was baptized.

Like the Old City of Jerusalem, the Jordan is almost too small to bear such a tremendous weight of history and devotion. When it flows from its source in Mount Hermon up north, it is wide enough, but when it reaches its southern destination in Judea, where John the Baptist baptized (John 3:23), it now narrows considerably. In biblical times, during the seasonal floods, it could be as much as a mile across. Now, with the damming of the river, it can be as little as thirty-three feet wide. For some this is a problem for their piety, since they suppose a river of such immense significance must surely be wider across. The first sight of the Jordan must be somewhat disappointing for those arriving with such an expectation.

But the size of Jerusalem had already prepared me for such mathematics, and I now knew better than to equate spiritual immensity with physical size. I therefore did not mind that the Jordan River was only about thirty-three feet across. More important was the fact that this water had been flowing for centuries and that its current had washed past the feet of the Savior. Others evidently felt this too.

When my companion and I arrived at the sacred stream, other Christian groups were already there, including other

Orthodox (I recognized the priest's cassock) and a Pentecostal group (I recognized the upraised hands and the guitars). We joined them, going past the armed Israeli soldier overlooking the site (crossing the river meant leaving Israel and entering the neighboring nation of Jordan—*not* advised), and went down to the place provided for pilgrims. Like everyone else who has ever visited the sacred stream, I took off my shoes and socks and waded in, washing myself in its waters. My companion and I sang the Theophany troparion, and I imagined John the Forerunner standing just downstream. Later on, sitting dry and comfortable back in our apartment, I asked myself why.

It is not that the Jordan's water is sacramental in the sense that baptism is sacramental. Unless one is actually being baptized in the Jordan, its water is just water; it cannot bestow new birth and remission of sins any more than can any other water in Israel. But in a sense *all* of the Holy Land is sacramental, for everything there points away from itself and toward higher realities. The place is living typology, its every shoreline rock soaked in holy history. For the devout pilgrim, the Bible with all its narrative and prophecy is not just a history book. The Bible is also geography, a place where one can walk.

Since time did not stop when the writing of the biblical text was finished at the end of the first century, and since the Holy Land continued to be occupied by someone throughout all the centuries (until 1948, by the Arabs, living in a land they called Palestine), naturally the Holy Land has undergone some changes since the death of the last apostle. Throughout the years, Christians have worshipped at its sacred sites and adorned them as best they could. They have lived in its cities, done business there, and built schools there. Its towns and cities therefore look like any other modern town, and not much like the towns of the first century. We are more likely to see taxi drivers than shepherds, more likely to see shops selling Coca-Cola than nomads riding camels.

The world of the first century and even of Byzantium lies buried in the Holy Land. But this veil separating us from the earlier time we long to see and touch wears thin when we come to the Jordan. Its width may have contracted of late, but in every other way it looks pretty much as it did when John the Baptist strode into its stream and baptized the Lamb of God. That is why people who come there wade into the water and pour it over their faces. Here at last is something biblical that the passage of time and the growth of modern civilization haven't altered.

The Jordan's water may not be, strictly speaking, drinkable (there are signs warning the pilgrim not to try), but it can quench the inner thirst to connect with the past and seems to wash away the accumulation of centuries. When I stood in the Jordan with the water up to my knees and splashed the water over my face and shoulders, I felt younger than I had for years. It was with the greatest regret that I stepped back to the shore, put on my shoes, and trudged slowly back to the waiting taxi.

~: 5 :~

Bethany and Wadi Qelt

The Tomb of Lazarus, Bethany

[On Lazarus Saturday] the archdeacon makes this announcement: "At one o'clock today let us all be ready at the Lazarium." Just on one o'clock everyone arrives at the Lazarium, which is in Bethany, about two miles away from the city. About half a mile before you get to the Lazarium from Jerusalem there is a church by the road. It is the spot where Lazarus's sister Mary met the Lord. All the monks meet the bishop when he arrives there and the people go into the church, they have one hymn and an antiphon and a reading

> *from the Gospel, then after a prayer, everyone is blessed and they go on with singing to the Lazarium. By the time they arrive there so many people have collected that they fill not only the Lazarium itself but all the field around. They have hymns and antiphons which are suitable to the day and the place.*
>
> EGERIA, CHAPTER 29, DESCRIBING THE SERVICES ON LAZARUS SATURDAY IN BETHANY

Bethany is very close to Jerusalem—so close that after our Lord entered Jerusalem and cleansed the Temple during the final week of His life, He "went out of the city to Bethany, and He lodged there" (Matt. 21:17), probably staying with Mary and Martha and Lazarus (John 12:1). Bethany is thus an easy walk from Jerusalem and used to be an even shorter drive.

But not anymore. The taxi driver contracted to drive us around the Holy Land to such places had to take a much longer way around since the Israelis built their wall separating Bethany from Jerusalem. Formerly anyone wanting to walk in our Lord's footsteps could trace His easy way from Bethany to Jerusalem; now the path connecting Bethany to Jerusalem detours far afield to get around the wall. As I looked up at that formidable thirty-foot barrier and listened to my Christian Arab driver tell us stories of what it was like to live there as an Arab, and of how more and more Jewish settlements were being illegally built on Palestinian land, I thought that the wall was a greater barrier than many realized. We succeeded in driving around it and arrived at our destination in Bethany. But it would not be so easy for Israeli and Arab in that troubled land to arrive at a place of peace.

The raising of Lazarus (narrated at length in John 11:1–44) formed the crown and climax of Christ's miracles. Out of the many miracles Christ performed, St. John deliberately chose seven of them to relate, and last was the raising of Lazarus. It was the most public and spectacular of the Lord's works, eclipsing even His prior miracles of resurrection. When He raised from the dead the son of the widow of Nain (Luke 7:11–17) or the young daughter of Jairus (Mark 5:35–43), He did this shortly after the death of the deceased (since in that hot climate, the dead were always buried on the same day they died).

But the raising of Lazarus was different, for the Lord waited until he had been dead and buried for four days before raising him (John 11:39), when decomposition would already have set in. That is, Lazarus had already begun to rot, and it was no wonder that when the Lord commanded the stone be taken away from the door of the tomb, the practical Martha protested there would be an intolerable stench (v. 39). This made the miracle all the more astonishing, for it involved not simply returning the spirit to the now-reanimated body, but also turning back all the forces of decay that had begun working within the corpse. It was a complete remaking of the body, and as such, a fit image of the final resurrection of all people on the Last Day, when the Lord's voice would call everyone from their tombs (John 5:28–29). No wonder Jesus described it as a manifestation of "the glory of God" (11:40). No wonder that when the people saw this sign, many believed in Him (v. 45).

Given the magnitude and magnificence of this final miracle, the actual site is disappointing and a bit depressing, for it is not within a church but a mosque, and of course lacks the dignity and adornment befitting such a Christian shrine. As with the chapel of the Ascension, the present Muslim owners have not seen fit to beautify a Christian site. Christian churches lie close by, but the tomb of Lazarus remains in Muslim hands. Egeria found a spacious and beautiful church; we found a building marked only with a dingy orange sign saying "Lazarus tomb" and another placard asking that visitors kindly show it some respect. I thought that signs pointing the way to restroom facilities in airports had greater elegance than these signs, which grudgingly identified the undistinguished site to persevering pilgrims.

The tomb itself is now reached by descending a steep set of steps, built by the Franciscans soon after 1610, climbing backward as if on a ladder. (This makes the annual procession to the tomb by the Christians of the Russian Orthodox Church Outside Russia on Lazarus Saturday very difficult also, for the climb cannot be performed with any liturgical grace.) In its present state the tomb itself is reached by first entering an antechamber, rather like the antechamber of the Lord's tomb (the so-called "chapel of the angels"). Once in this antechamber, one must crawl again through a kind of manhole in the floor to reach the tomb of Lazarus. Some have suggested that originally both the tomb and its antechamber were on the same level, but that with the passage of years limestone from the ceiling fell down and thus raised the level of the antechamber.

There is nothing remotely devotional about the site, reached after much effort. We climbed down and down and came to rest at the bottom, finding there absolutely nothing of note. My companion and I did our best to sanctify it by singing the troparion for Lazarus Saturday, "By raising Lazarus from the dead before Your Passion, You confirmed the universal resurrection, O Christ God." We then emerged into the light of day and left the tomb to its present obscurity, for its present location behind the barrier wall means that many pilgrims no longer visit there.

It was not always so. As seen above, in Egeria's day, there was a splendid church there, the Lazarium. On Lazarus Saturday, she reports that multitudes of people meet together and "go on with singing to the Lazarium. By the time they arrive there so many people have collected that they fill not only the Lazarium itself, but all the fields around" (ch. 29). The church there was built at a sixty-degree angle to a tomb, not at right angles, suggesting that the tomb was indeed the tomb of Lazarus, used as a place of Christian pilgrimage even before the church was built in the fourth century, and that the church accommodated itself to this tomb. Entrance to the original site and tomb was through the courtyard of the church.

As I reflected on the present dreary state of this formerly glorious Christian site, I thought of how the Lazarium had come to endure the same fate as Lazarus himself, and that perhaps that was not altogether a bad thing. Lazarus had his moment of glory, shining in the reflected glory of the One who raised him from the dead. When Jesus sat at supper in Bethany after that miracle, "a great many of the Jews knew that He was there; and they came, not for Jesus' sake only, but that they might also see Lazarus, whom He had raised from the dead" (John 12:9). In the Pentecostal growth of the church that followed in the coming months, no doubt Lazarus was something of a celebrity, applauded by the Christians and hated by the Jews. One tradition reports that Jewish hostility forced him to flee his native Palestine and take refuge in Kition, in Cyprus (now modern Larnaka), being appointed bishop there by Paul and Barnabas.

There is nothing terribly unlikely about this; Barnabas had family connections there, which perhaps explains why he and Paul went there on their first apostolic journey (Acts 4:36; 13:4). After he died there, Lazarus's relics were translated to Constantinople in 898 (the imperial city had a penchant for centralizing such relics) and from there were stolen by the Crusaders when they sacked the city in 1204 and carried with them to Marseilles. This latter perhaps accounts for the Western medieval tradition that Mary, Martha, and Lazarus were set adrift in a boat by the Jews and ended up in France, whereupon Lazarus went to preach in Marseilles. Whatever the value of such traditions, it is certain that Lazarus, after being raised to life by Christ in Bethany, later died again. It is said by some that from the time Christ raised him until his final death, he never smiled, remembering the plight of those in Hades, where he dwelt for four days.

So, after Lazarus's moment of earthly glory, he eventually died again, and the church named after him in Bethany shared this fate, for after the Lazarium's moment of Byzantine glory came its Islamic eclipse and prolonged decay. Lazarus and his tomb reveal that in this age, all ends in the dust of death, and the weight of centuries will one day cover us all. Lazarus now awaits a second and final resurrection, a rising that will never end in corruption, a day that will never know evening. We all wait with him for that final triumph and need not fear when our earthly happiness fades. As we wait to hear the same Voice that summoned him from the dust, we need not fear whatever disasters may befall us, nor be distressed if we live in Bethany. For us as for Lazarus, all will end in glory.

St. George's Monastery in Wadi Qelt and St. Gerasimus Monastery

*We traveled through the Jordan valley for a little
and at times the road took us along the river bank*

itself. Then Tishbe came in sight, the city from which the holy prophet Elijah gets his name "the Tishbite." To this day they have there the cave in which he lived. So we gave thanks to God there in our usual way and set off once more. As we went on we saw a very well kept valley coming down towards us on the left. It was very large, and had a good-sized stream in it which ran down into the Jordan. In this valley was the cell of a brother, a monk. You know how inquisitive I am, and I asked what there was about this valley to make this holy monk build his cell there. This is what I was told by the holy men with us who knew the district: "This is the valley of Cherith."

EGERIA, CHAPTER 16, DESCRIBING
THE WILDERNESS WHERE
ELIJAH HAD HIS CAVE

After Bethany, my companion was eager to return to Wadi Qelt, a forbidding part of the Judean wilderness. (*Wadi* is the Arabic term for a valley, usually denoting a dry riverbed that flows with water only during the time of torrential rains.) The monastery near this wadi, now known as St. George's Monastery, is about twelve and a half miles from Jerusalem as one approaches Jericho. One tradition regards it as the "valley of the shadow of death" made famous by the twenty-third psalm. It certainly looks the part and is approached on foot on a long and winding road. The monastery now clings to the bare rock face, where it welcomes pilgrims brave enough to make the long and demanding hike. It is named after one of its most famous inhabitants, St. George the Chozebite, who was born in Cyprus toward the end of the sixth century and went to Palestine, where he eventually became the head of the community here. I confess that I did not share his enthusiasm for visiting the place; my companion described the arduous approach to it very vividly.

It was well that he was not deterred by my lack of enthusiasm, for the place exceeds expectation in every way. Whether or not it holds the actual cave used by Elijah in 1 Kings 17:2–7 (there are a lot of caves in the wadi, and ancient Jewish memory had no incentive to determine exactly which one was his), there is no denying that the ascetic spirit of Elijah still animates the place. The rocks were full of caves, tiny holes used by desert-dwelling monks as their austere quarters, chosen by them for their austerity. The desert thus became a city, and its rocks resounded with the prayers and chanting of the hermits. It is a hard and unforgiving place, a place defying human habitation, a place hard enough to shatter man's comfortable complacence. In its ungenerous landscape, a man knows he can only be sustained by divine care; in its endless silence, he can hear the voice of God. The men who made this their home must indeed have been angels in the flesh and men of fire.

When faced with such extraordinary exploits, we are tempted to distance ourselves from such men and to assume that they were utterly unlike us. We want to admire them from afar and conclude that such efforts in ascetic holiness are the exclusive preserve of monks and desert dwellers, and that we who live with families in the city are exempt. *They* can fast and pray and devour Scripture and mourn over their sins. We will simply go to church and light a few candles. After all, such desert dwellers were not men of like nature with ourselves. We will classify them safely as saints, venerate their images, admire their exploits, and carry on our way.

In fact, Elijah and his successors there *were* men "with a nature like ours" (James 5:17), and we have no right to regard their monastery as a kind of quarantine that keeps them and their example at a safe distance from us. It is true, of course, that it is unlikely we could ever imitate their deeds, sever all earthly ties, and live for God in the lonely rocks. It is also true that I could never run as fast or jump as high as those who win Olympic gold medals for running and jumping. But that does not mean that because I watch the Olympics and applaud the Olympians' speed, I am somehow off the hook and needn't go jogging. Olympic athletes in fact perform their exploits partly to inspire the rest of us, and the gold medalist hockey player inspires thousands of kids to get up off the couch and go outside to play hockey.

In the same way, the saints of St. George's Monastery and the Wadi Qelt serve to inspire the rest of us. God does not give them to the rest of us as exceptions, but as exemplars. We are meant to see them fasting and praying ceaselessly in the barren wilderness and conclude that perhaps we can fast and pray a little more in our suburban homes. If St. George could eat but once a day, perhaps I can keep the Lenten fast more strictly. If he could keep prayerful vigil, standing throughout the long hours of the night, perhaps I could pray a little more in my prayer corner. We need the monks in the wilderness, not only as intercessors for the Church and the world, but also as relentless reminders that sanctity is incumbent upon all the people of God, and that all of us must strive for the "holiness without which no one will see the Lord" (Heb. 12:14).

The Monastery of St. George in the Wadi Qelt contrasts dramatically with the next site we visited, the Monastery of St. Gerasimus, west of the Jordan River. My companion especially was eager to visit here, since it was once the home of St. Gerasimus, who settled there in the fifth century. He is famous for befriending a distressed lion (they once abounded in Palestine) and removing a thorn from its paw. The beast took a liking to its benefactor and followed Gerasimus home to his monastic dwelling, becoming something of a beloved fixture there among the monks. When Gerasimus at length died and was buried, the lion went all over the monastery grounds seeking his master and was only dissuaded from further searching when the monks led the beast to the grave where Gerasimus had just been interred. The lion thereupon disconsolately stretched itself out on the grave and refused to move, dying there from grief. Gerasimus had named the lion Jordan, after the nearby river, and it lives on in all the saint's icons.

With such love and admiration for St. Gerasimus beating in our hearts, we were unprepared for the current state of the monastery bearing his name. No monks could be found. But we did find a shop selling ice cream and cosmetics. (Yep, cosmetics, Dead Sea cosmetics. Care for some aromatic body butter and luxurious perfume oil? Only $62 for 350 ml, available also online.) My friend commented that all that was lacking to complete the picture of decadent Disneyesque secularization were pony rides. No sooner had he uttered the fateful words than we found them too—donkey rides actually, available for the visiting children.

Presumably the church authorities feel these measures are necessary to keep the church open (hoping for better spiritual times?) and so acquiesce in its present debasement. But even so, the contrast between the severe asceticism of its founder and his church's present condition is stunning. I was a bit surprised to see such decadence. My diaconal companion was depressed. He had come hoping to find true monasticism blooming like a flower in the desert. Instead he found cosmetics and donkey rides. When we took the candles that were offered us there, I decided I would give them to the children of our Sunday school when we returned home. Better to look to the future than to mourn the past.

The contrast between the two monasteries offers a cautionary tale and tells us that even when the fire has been extinguished from an institution, the empty shell remains. Institutions, whether they be monasteries, church denominations, or organizations, can go through cycles of vigor and weakness, of fidelity to their original vision and betrayal of it, of life and death. Sometimes out of respect or nostalgia for the original vision, people persist in propping up the institution—especially if jobs or a flow of money are dependent upon their continued existence. Institutions have lives of their own, being deliberately constructed to outlast their founders. They thus resist being shut down and persist long after they have ceased to bear much resemblance to their first state. But such institutional persistence and longevity come with a hidden cost, for they lower the bar for everyone and serve to redefine a new normal.

We all know, for example, of organizations once committed to renewal that have long since ceased to renew. What is perhaps less obvious is that their continued existence redraws the spiritual map and rewrites the spiritual glossary, so that "renewal" now means not what it did before, but the lesser reality it has now become. Those being thus "renewed" have a different expectation and no longer aspire to what their fathers once experienced. They are therefore doubly cut off from the possibility of attaining to the higher realities once experienced as normal.

In the desert around Jericho, men once thought it normal to fast all day and pray for hours at a time. They fled from entertainment and from the fleeting beauty of the world to seek the lasting beauty of the Kingdom. Whether or not we can reach the height they reached, that height still remains as the standard. It would be tragic for ancient monastic institutions to die out; but it would be more tragic still to allow them to persist at the cost of lowering the perennial standard that was the reason for their existence.

St. George the Chozebite and St. Gerasimus of the Jordan alike knew that what mattered was not the communities they founded but the fidelity of those communities to the Gospel. The monastery buildings were simply the fireplace, and they existed for no other purpose but to burn with spiritual fire and to give us warmth and light. It is sad to come to the fireplace now and find only the ashes of a blaze long spent.

~: 6 :~

Outside the Walls
St. Stephen's & Siloam

Outside the walls of the Old City, we went next to visit St. Stephen's Church, a beautiful Orthodox church with a "martyrion" outside, a grotto that purports to mark the exact spot where Stephen was martyred. The church's location presupposes that Stephen was hustled out after his trial through the Lion Gate of the Old City (later renamed in his honor St. Stephen's Gate) and then stoned to death. The present church was built on the site of the church built by the Empress Eudokia in the fifth century to house the relics of St. Stephen.

The grotto is found next to the church and is not very visible to the casual observer. In fact we would have missed it entirely were it not for the kindness of someone in the church itself inviting us to visit the grotto as well. The church was largely empty, and the grotto more deserted still, for the church and its martyrion have experienced the decline that has befallen Christianity generally in the land of its birth, and few now come to venerate the place where Stephen witnessed to Christ with the shedding of his blood. The empty grotto did, however, give us ample opportunity to pray and reflect on Stephen's martyrdom.

It is possible, however, that though the site marks the reliquary church keeping Stephen's remains, it does not mark the actual place of his martyrdom. Another, early tradition asserts that Stephen was hustled out of the city not through the Lion Gate, but through the Damascus Gate. A distinction between the place of his relics and the place of his martyrdom could quickly become lost, so that people seeing the church housing Stephen's relics could assume that it also marked the place of his martyrdom. The New Testament text in Acts 6–7 simply doesn't indicate where he was killed. We cannot even be sure, when they "brought *him* to the council" (Acts 6:12), where this council met, much less by what route they would have hustled him out of the city. It is possible the trial of Stephen took place in the Temple precincts (hence the reference to the Temple on the part of the false witnesses as "this holy place" in Acts 6:13). If that were the case, the Lion Gate would indeed have been close by. But certainty continues to evade us.

Ultimately, of course, the actual spot of his martyrdom is not important. The place where the church was built became a nexus between heaven and earth, a place where Stephen's final words were read and where gratitude to him was poured out. For Stephen was not simply the first martyr. He was a boundary, and the blood that flowed from his body during his stoning became a river separating the faith of the Christians from the religion of Judaism.

St. Stephen is rightly hailed as the Protomartyr, the first in a long line of men and women who would lay down their lives for Christ in the coming centuries. Most of these martyrs prior to the Peace of Constantine were killed, because Christianity was then an illegal religion. The Roman law was clear enough: Christians were not allowed to exist, and if one publicly acknowledged that one was indeed a member of the Christian Church, the Roman authorities accepted this as a guilty plea to a capital offense. Execution followed, usually, immediately.

Stephen, however, was a different case. In his day, the Christian Faith was not illegal under Roman law, and in fact the Romans rescued Paul when he was in mortal danger from his Jewish compatriots. What then was Stephen's crime? What did he say to so enrage his listeners that they ground their teeth against him and lynched him (Acts 7:54–58)?

The false witnesses at his trial said that Stephen "does not cease to speak blasphemous words against this holy place [i.e. the Temple] and the law; for we have heard him say that this Jesus of Nazareth will destroy this place and will change the customs which Moses delivered to us" (Acts 6:13–14). Some of these allegations had been heard before: At the trial of Jesus, some false witnesses said He claimed He would destroy the Temple made with hands and in three days build another, made without hands (Mark 14:58). This is clearly a misremembered utterance—what Christ actually said was that if His foes would destroy this temple, in three days He would raise it up (obviously referring to the raised temple of His body; John 2:19–21). But the misquote stuck, and His foes continued to assert that Jesus was threatening to destroy the Temple.

Despite the garbled form of the testimony, there was a kernel of truth in what the false witnesses against Stephen said. For although Jesus never spoke against the Temple or the Law, He did clearly regard them differently than did His Jewish adversaries, and this was Stephen's main message. Nationhood, Temple, and Law were paramount in Judaism, and Jews thought they needed all of them. The Messiah was thus subordinate to the Temple and the Law; his messianic task was to support them. Stephen's point (as was apparent from his defense in Acts 7) was that the Temple was never paramount in the history of God's people, for from the days of Abraham onward, they were to be a pilgrim people, a people on the move—hence the portable tent shrine established under Moses. Moses did not command them to build the Temple. The Temple was not even built during David's reign. That immense and immovable structure only came with Solomon.

The movability of the original tent shrine revealed God's

intention that His people be ever moving on and ever open to new truth—such as the new truth in Jesus. In Jesus, God was revealing a new phase in Israel's pilgrimage through history, a phase in which Temple and Law and City were no longer needed. In Jesus these old realities had been radically relativized and made subordinate to Him.

Jesus did not say He would destroy the Temple, but He did act in such a way that the Temple was not necessary: when He spoke to the Samaritan woman, for example, He said that neither on her Mount Gerizim nor at the Temple in Jerusalem would men worship the Father (John 4:21f). Times were changing, and the Father would now be worshipped in the Spirit and in the truth (i.e. the truth of the Gospel). Men would still enter the Temple to offer sacrifice (compare the practice of the apostles in Acts 21:23–26), but these sacrifices were now of more cultural significance than covenantal. The definitive Temple, the locus of sacrifice and praise and salvation, now was Jesus. Judaism as a religion had been transcended and was to give place to Christianity. Messiah in this new understanding was not subordinate to Judaism with its Law and Temple; rather, they were subordinate to Him.

This understanding struck at the heart of all that the Jewish adversaries of Stephen valued. For them, faith in God was unthinkable without Law and Temple as ultimate realities. The Jewish state and its capital at Jerusalem existed to protect the Temple and keep it secure. Stephen's words therefore threatened their whole world—and this at a time when things with the Romans were beginning to heat up. The Zealot movement was gaining ground, and their political assassinations in the decades leading up to AD 70 were one of the reasons the Romans decided to destroy the Temple and end the Jewish state. In this heated atmosphere, the words of Stephen must have appeared all the more dangerous.

Stephen, though the first martyr, would not be the last, for he would soon be joined by a host of others—Peter and Paul in Rome a few decades later, Ignatius the bishop of Antioch, dying in about 107, and Polycarp bishop of Smyrna, dying in the middle of the second century. But Stephen's death was different. He was one of the first to see that faith in Jesus of Nazareth changed everything; it could not be contained within Judaism as if it were just another Jewish sect, its fortunes dependent upon those of the Jewish state.

In Hebrews 13:12 we read that Jesus "suffered outside the gate," meaning that as Jesus was cast out of the city through its gates and died outside the city, so those who believe in Him must follow Him outside the confines of Judaism. St. Stephen, suffering outside the city gates, understood this and blazed the way for us as well. The tenacity with which he clung to this vision of the Christian Faith, even to death, helped the Church of the first century know what it was: not just another species of Judaism, but a faith large enough to contain the world.

As I stood in the martyrion commemorating the place of his

martyrdom, I thought of how much we owe to St. Stephen for his courage and the clarity of his vision. When Stephen shed his blood for his Master, he was surrounded by those who hated him and whose faces were contorted with rage as they shrieked at him and hurled stones. It was good to stand in this place of peace, erected by those who loved him and who wanted to honor his witness. Before I left, I knelt to kiss the ground on which Stephen may have trod during his final hours on this earth.

Siloam

After visiting St. Stephen's Church, my companion and I next walked the long, steep way down from the city gates to the site of the pool of Siloam, located to the southeast of the old city of David, well outside the present walls of the Old City. The pool is famous as the site of our Lord's healing of the man born blind, narrated in John 9. The pool has a long history and a confused one. The walk was long, and all downhill, and at every step my aged knees complained. It gave me time to think about the healing that happened there.

The source of the pool is the Gihon spring, which was the main water source for Jerusalem from before the time of David. The name Siloam is from the Hebrew *shiloah*, meaning "sent," since the water there was *sent* from the Gihon spring. This pool is known as the lower pool. There was also nearby another pool, the upper pool, built by Hezekiah to be within the defensive walls of the city in the late eighth century BC. Scholars still argue about which pool was the one to which Jesus sent the blind man to wash. Christians since before the middle of the fourth century thought the upper pool was the authentic one. Some archeologists now seem to be suggesting that the lower pool was the one mentioned in the Gospel. Fortunately, understanding the Gospel story does not require solving this scholarly question.

Since much of the Gospel of John takes place in the Temple (2:14–20; 7:14–38; 8:2–59; 10:22–38), some assume that Christ first found the man in the Temple and sent him out on his long trek down the road to the distant Pool of Siloam—all the longer a trek for a blind man. But there is nothing in the text to suggest that Christ first found him in the Temple. The text in John 9:1 simply says, "as Jesus passed by, He saw a man who was blind from birth," and the story reads most naturally if it took place near the pool.

The story is concisely told in John's Gospel. As He passed by, Christ saw the man, blind from birth, and had compassion on him. No doubt the man sat begging in the same place day after day and was a well-known fixture. The Lord did not wait for the man to ask for His help; it is doubtful he could have known that the person standing close by was Jesus. Jesus spat on the ground, made clay from the dirt and spittle, and smeared the mud on the man's eyes. The man doubtless was surprised at this sudden assault on his eyes, though he seems to have learned that Jesus was the one smearing the stuff on. Jesus then told him to go and wash it off in the nearby pool of Siloam. "So he went and washed, and came back seeing" (John 9:7).

We can imagine the man, his heart pounding, climbing and stumbling down the steps to the water, and bending over to wash the mud off. And the moment of sight! Since he had been born blind, he had never seen color, or birds, or the mountains, or the Temple, or a human face. At that instant, a whole wide world opened before him, flooding in through his eyes and into his heart. Doubtless he rushed back to the place where he had sat begging before, but by then Jesus had gone.

It was not until later, after he had been cross-examined minutely by Jesus' foes and been cast out of the synagogue for siding with Jesus, that he again found his benefactor. When Jesus heard they had cast the man out for siding with Him, He found him and said, "Do you believe in the Son of Man?" The man answered, "Who is He, Lord, that I may believe in Him?" Jesus replied, "You have both seen Him and it is He who is talking to you." The man's eyes widened, and he fell down before Christ, saying, "Lord, I believe" (John 9:35–38).

The story is interesting not only for what it tells us about the miracle and its immediate aftermath, but also for what it tells us about our own baptism. Jesus did not need to smear mud on the man's eyes and command him to wash it off in the nearby pool. In fact, His use of such a pool in His healing ministry was very unusual. Usually Jesus simply laid hands upon the sick to heal them (Mark 6:5). One time, when healing a deaf and dumb man,

He put His fingers into his ears, spat upon His fingers, and then touched the man's tongue (Mark 7:33). Often He healed with a simple word, only telling the needy persons to go their way, and healing took place as they went (Mark 7:29; Luke 17:14; John 4:50).

This use of water is almost unprecedented, but I don't think it is accidental. John wants us to see this miracle as an image of baptism. He makes a point of translating for his Greek readers the meaning of the Hebrew *shiloah/siloam*, saying that it meant "sent." The blind man received his sight and a brand new life by washing in the pool of the Sent. As part of the man's new life, he prostrates before Jesus, saying, "Lord, I believe"—an utterance Christians of the first century could hardly have failed to identify as a baptismal confession. Thus illumination comes through washing in the pool of the Sent One (compare John 6:29), the baptismal font of Christ. And ever after, baptism was regarded in the Church as illumination and enlightenment (compare Eph. 5:14; Heb. 6:4).

The little bits of the lower pool that still exist obscure rather than reveal how it must have looked when our Lord sent the blind man there to wash. A guide there suggested to us that most of the original pool was now under an orchard owned by the Greek Orthodox and as yet unexcavated. My constant historical itch to find the precise spot thus could find no satisfaction. I told myself that somewhere near here, perhaps a stone's throw away, the man stooped into the water, and washed, and saw.

As I stood and stared at the excavations going on at the pool of Siloam, I thought of the baptismal font of our own little church many thousands of miles away. If every Christian font is a kind of Jordan, it is also a pool of Siloam. In it, those who are spiritually blind from birth can come and wash and go away enlightened, able now to see new spiritual realities and live a brand new life.

~: 7 :~

Galilee

Our trip to Galilee began very early. It also began with a taxi ride. The days we had set apart to visit Galilee fell within the Jewish Feast of Weeks, Shavuot, and the usual buses were not running. I am told these restrictions are even more severe during Yom Kippur, the Day of Atonement, so that if you need anything commercial during this time you are spectacularly out of luck. We were therefore all the happier to have a taxi to take us up north to Galilee. It was a quick trip, for we were determined to see all we could of Galilee during one long day.

I was surprised that the journey on the highway from Jerusalem to Galilee took only about two and a half hours by car, including slowing for traffic and for stops. All my life I had been looking at maps of the Holy Land and comparing them unconsciously with maps of my own Canada or of the United

States. The distance between Jerusalem and Galilee showed up as about three inches on my Holy Land map, and a corresponding three inches on my map of Canada represented hundreds of miles. Of course I knew intellectually that Canada was much larger than Palestine and that therefore the inches on a map were not comparable, but it took the actual journey to bring this home to me. The journey to Mount Tabor was about 98 miles, the approximate distance from Toronto, Ontario, to Buffalo, New York. Our Lord walked a similar journey, going from up north to Bethany, in about two days (see John 11:6, 17).

Mount Tabor

Mount Tabor is famous as the traditional site of the Transfiguration, and Orthodox often speak of the Lord's transfigured glory as "the light of Tabor." The New Testament text, however, does not specify which mountain our Lord ascended. It simply says that He led Peter, James, and John up "a high mountain" (Matt. 17:1; Mark 9:2; Luke 9:28). Some have suggested that Tabor could not possibly be the correct site, since there were residences and a Roman garrison there at the time. They propose Mount Hermon as an alternative site. This approach wants to link the location of the Transfiguration with Caesarea-Philippi, since the apostles' confession of Christ at Caesarea-Philippi is narrated just before the account of the Transfiguration. If the two sites must be close to one another, then Mount Hermon is indeed closer to Caesarea-Philippi than is Mount Tabor. But no such proximity is required. Matthew's Gospel explicitly says that the events of Transfiguration happened "after six days" (Matt. 17:1)—plenty of time for our Lord to move from Caesarea-Philippi back to His base in Galilee.

The problem with Mount Hermon as the correct site is, I suggest, that it was too far away. The Gospels say that after the events of the Transfiguration, Christ descended the mountain the next morning (Luke 9:37) and met a gathered crowd. This crowd must have been in Galilee, for the text next mentions them gathering in Galilee (Matt. 17:22) and then returning at last to their base in Capernaum (Matt. 17:24). The distance from Mount Hermon to the towns of Galilee is about forty miles as the crow flies—too great a distance to travel in such a short time.

On the other hand, the distance from Mount Tabor to the towns of Galilee is only a few miles—rather easier to cover in a morning. The narrative reads most naturally as if the post-Transfiguration meeting in Galilee happened early the next day—not time enough to travel from Mount Hermon, but a journey easily made from Mount Tabor. And if their ministry was mostly in Galilee, one asks why they would make the journey to distant Hermon when Tabor was right there, dominating the landscape. The presence of residences or of a Roman garrison on the summit of Tabor would have been no impediment to the Transfiguration occurring there. Tabor is a large mountain, with plenty of space for four men to camp somewhere on it overnight and not be disturbed.

Anyway, we ascended Mount Tabor, driving up the winding road. There we visited the two churches of Mount Tabor, the Roman Catholic one and the Orthodox one. This pattern was repeated throughout the Holy Land, as the Latin West and the Orthodox East strove with each other, often making competing claims to have the authentic site of biblical events, each asserting itself as the true heir of Scripture and church history. The rival claims to be the true and original Church were expressed in wood and stone, and time and again we found at the holy sites buildings belonging to Roman Catholicism or to Orthodoxy. It was instructive to compare the buildings, for they say much about the churches and faiths to which they belong.

The Roman Catholic Church of the Transfiguration, though it dates from 1924, is built on the site of the older Byzantine and Crusader churches. It is a beautiful church, with the elegant simplicity that the classic West does so well. When we arrived, a Mass was going on. Above it all, a glorious mosaic of the Transfiguration beamed down upon the worshippers.

The Orthodox rival is dedicated to St. Elias, who appeared with Moses and Christ on Mount Tabor at the Transfiguration. The church was built in 1845 on the site of an earlier Crusader church, with some of its iconography added in 1912. Its interior is breathtaking, with every inch covered by icons. It was also the home of an icon of the Theotokos reputed to be wonderworking, and indeed we saw the customary tokens of answered prayer hanging from it.

The contrast between the two churches was striking, for one could take in at a glance the beautiful and splendid simplicity of the Roman Catholic Church, but would need hours to fully absorb the gorgeous detail filling the Orthodox one. Also, the Orthodox locale was the shrine containing the miraculous icon.

The glory of detail in this church's iconography mirrors the interior richness of the Orthodox faith, a richness able to engage and capture the human heart, and which can call forth the power of God—hence the wonderworking icon within the church.

There is no compelling reason to think either the Roman Catholic or the Orthodox church marks the actual spot of the Transfiguration. Our ancestors were practical people, and in the absence of any secure memory locating the actual spot, the first churches there were built with other factors in mind. Popular piety often demands to know the actual spot where sacred events occurred, and sometimes local churches acquiesce in meeting that demand, even in the complete absence of evidence. But what remains important is the meaning of the sacred event itself, not our ability to mark it on a map.

One night, somewhere on this mountain of Tabor, the apostles awoke to see their Lord transfigured, shining with the glory that was rightly His. No doubt this is how the angels and demons always saw Him; it would explain why the demons cried out with fear whenever He approached (Mark 3:11). Seeing this private revelation of His messianic glory, the apostles knew He was indeed the Messiah, and the vision on Mount Tabor thus confirmed their confession at Caesarea-Philippi. It also revealed what being the Messiah meant—not a conquering hero, but a lamb slain to take away the sins of the world.

On that mountain, Christ spoke with Elias and Moses about His "exodus" (Luke 9:31), His departure, which He would accomplish at Jerusalem. This was the advance proof to the disciples that Christ's death on the Cross was the fulfillment of His own will. His enemies did not succeed in killing Him when He wanted to remain alive. It might have looked that way to the populace when He was arrested, tried, and executed, but the truth was deeper and more wonderful. No one took His life from Him; He laid it down of His own accord (John 10:18). The Taborite churches, each beautiful in its own way, stood as lasting architectural witnesses to that revelation.

After we had driven down the mountain and were hastening along the road to our next Galilean destination, I could look back and see the mountain in the near distance. Oddly enough, I found this sight to be more devotional than my visits to the two churches. The churches were lovely, each in its own way, but there was nothing particularly Taborite within them, nothing that could not be found in any church dedicated to the Transfiguration. But seeing the mountain itself dominating the area, rising above the quiet fields below, I felt the sanctity of the place and its abiding connection with the events recorded in the Gospels. As we drove away, I could hold up my hand and frame the whole mountain within my fingers. Somewhere on that hill Christ encamped with His disciples and startled them with His transfigured glory.

I felt closer to the events as we drove away. I looked out the window back at the hill for a long time. I tried to take a photo of the hill from our moving vehicle, with predictable results. But the image still remains in my memory, vivid, clear, and precious.

Nazareth

> *There is a big and very splendid cave in which [holy Mary] lived. An altar has been placed there, and within the actual cave is the place from which she drew water. Inside the city the synagogue where the Lord read the book of Isaiah is now a church, but the spring from which holy Mary used to take water is outside the village.*
>
> EGERIA, DESCRIBING THE CHURCH
> AND WELL IN NAZARETH

We next drove to Nazareth, about nine miles away. I had long wanted to come here, and when my traveling companion first asked me what I wanted to see in the Holy Land apart from the Church of the Holy Sepulcher, I instantly said, "Nazareth." He warned me that I would be disappointed.

He was thinking, I suppose, of the contrast between what every reader of the Bible imagines Nazareth to be like and the way it actually is. In the days of our Lord, Nazareth was a small hamlet of perhaps five hundred people. It was too small, and in fact is not mentioned once in the Old Testament.

When Matthew said the prophets prophesied, "He shall be called a Nazarene" (Matt. 2:23), he was dealing with the Scriptures in a typically Jewish way and making a play on words. Some prophets described the messianic King as a "branch." Thus Isaiah 11:1 says, "There shall come forth a Rod from the stem of Jesse, / And a Branch [Heb. *nezer*] shall grow out of his roots." Other prophets make the same point about the King arising as a struggling little branch, growing from the felled stump of the formerly great House of David (compare Jer. 23:5 and Zech. 3:8, though there a different Hebrew word for "branch" is used). The prophets were contrasting the former greatness of the House of David with the tiny new beginnings of the messianic King.

For Matthew, this tiny new beginning was expressed in the tiny size and social insignificance of Nazareth—mirrored in the actual name of the town, since the Hebrew word for "branch" sounded like the word "Nazareth." Nazareth was too small to show up on anyone's radar. Its insignificance was even proverbial—people from neighboring Cana would ask derisively, "Can anything good come out of Nazareth?" (John 1:46). When one arrived in Nazareth, there was practically nothing there to see.

My friend knew this was not the case now. Now there is lots

to see in Nazareth, which in 2009 was a city of 210,000 people, if you counted the greater Nazareth metropolitan area. The first thing we saw was traffic, with streets jammed with cars and thronging with people. There were modern shops and advertising, none of which remotely suggested the quiet and peaceful idyll years of Bible reading had indelibly etched into my brain. I was happy to ignore the traffic and the present city. I was looking for an earlier Nazareth, and when we stepped from our taxi into the Roman Catholic Church of the Annunciation, I thought I had found it.

The current church was built in 1969 over an earlier Byzantine site, which in turn was built around a cave purporting to be part of the home of the Virgin Mary. There is nothing unlikely about this, for Nazareth was a small enough hamlet in the days of Christ that there were not many homes from which to choose. If this were not the actual home of Mary, then it must have been nearby and looked rather like this, for many homes were then built over caves, which were used to house animals. Standing in the nave of the present church, one can see through a grille the grotto below, which contains the remnants of the old Byzantine church built around the residence of Mary. According to Roman Catholic tradition, the announcement of the angel Gabriel to her that she was to give birth to the Messiah occurred while she was at home—that is, in this very spot. One was not permitted to enter the grotto itself, but could only look through the grille, peering down through the centuries into the original house in which later generations had erected an altar. Staring into the grotto, I felt as if I were looking into the past down a deep well.

Not surprisingly, the Orthodox church in Nazareth, the church of St. Gabriel, sitting very nearby, nurtures a somewhat different and rival tradition regarding the place of the Annunciation. According to this tradition, the angelic announcement occurred not while Mary was at home, but while she was visiting the local well in Nazareth, and so the Greek Orthodox church was built to enclose that well.

The idea that the Annunciation took place at the well is rooted in the apocryphal second-century *Protoevangelium of James*, part of which says that Mary "took the jar and went out to fetch water. Then a voice spoke to her, 'Hail, you who have received grace. The Lord is with you, O blessed among women!' And she looked to the right and the left to see whence this voice came, and being filled with trembling she went to her house and set down the jar, and took the purple thread and sat down on her chair and drew out the thread [to sew the purple part of the veil for the Temple]. And behold, an angel of the Lord stood before her saying, 'Fear not, Mary, for you have found grace before the Lord.'"

As one can see, even by this account a case could be made for Mary's house as *the* location of the Annunciation. But for me the attraction of the well was not the fact that it marked the exact spot where Mary first heard the angelic voice, but the certainty that she had come here to use this very well, for in our Lord's time, this was the only well and water supply in Nazareth.

The Greek Orthodox church attached to the well is not as splendid as its Roman Catholic neighbor, and the iconography within is of varying styles and quality. The church is also much smaller. I did not spend much time inside it. I was mostly interested in the well, located down a few steps and along a corridor that connects to a site which, in our Lord's day, was of course above ground and near the center of the small village. I hurried down the hallway to the enclosed spring. I stood by the dimly lit well, gazed into it, used the little spigot provided to access its water, and poured some over my head. (A sign there said that drinking the water was not now advised.) I stared and stared into the well, into which coins had been thrown and around which hung many icons of the Theotokos. It took some imagination to return through the centuries and clear away the present buildings to stand once more in the open air of the first century, but it was worth the effort.

In our Lord's day, Nazareth was indeed smaller and correspondingly quieter. Everyone would have known everyone else in Nazareth. I imagined the current large city gone, its traffic gone, its shops and restaurants and shawarma sellers gone, its bustle and noise gone. I imagined it as a small hamlet nestled near the side of a wooded hill (Luke 4:29), home to humble and unimportant people, carpenters and artisans.

Mary lived a short walk from where I stood, even as the

present Roman Catholic basilica stood a short way from the Orthodox church. I could see her leaving the house with her water jar to go to the well and standing approximately where I was standing now, two thousand years later, drawing water. I thought of how the child Jesus would have accompanied her also sometimes during that daily ritual, and that someplace close by once knew the echo of their feet.

Then I looked around again and found myself standing in a busy Byzantine church, its intricately carved Cretan icon screen suffering decay. My dear friend and traveling companion was wrong. The bustle of the city and its crowded cluster of buildings did tax my imagination. But I was not disappointed in Nazareth.

Cana

For the Christian, the word *Cana* instantly summons up the story of Christ turning water into wine, as found in John 2:1–11. It might also summon up memories of Orthodox weddings, since Christ performed this miracle at a wedding, and this is the Gospel read at Orthodox wedding services. Our trip to Cana, or Kefr Kanna ("the village of Kanna"), included quick visits to the inevitable two rival sites, the Roman Catholic and the Orthodox one. They are both beautiful, and both display jars claiming to be among the original jars that held the water turned to wine (John 2:6). The town does a brisk tourist business, also selling (of course) "Cana wine," and boasts such places as "The First Miracle Wine's Shop [sic] and Souvenirs." I left not quite convinced that I was in the right place—or at least I thought if I were, Nathanael of Cana (mentioned in John 21:2) would be less than enthused about the present state of his old hometown.

The Roman Catholic church there looks very traditionally Catholic, complete with the usual statues (Mary is holding a rosary) and the Stations of the Cross, built by the Franciscans in the nineteenth century. People use it, not surprisingly, to renew their wedding vows, and it seems to do a reasonable business. (One website, "travelujah," bids one to "say 'I do' in the Holy Land.") The rival Orthodox church in Cana has two large stone containers purporting to be the original jars in which Christ turned the water to wine. One modern archaeologist argues more persuasively that they were originally baptismal fonts. After visiting both churches, I felt a tremendous desire to get away from the whole place as fast as possible. The commercialization of the entire town and its churches weighed upon me. Cana had come down in the world.

But it is just possible that Kefr Kanna is not the original Cana of Galilee. A number of voices are now being raised that suggest the best candidate for the ancient Cana is the ruined village of Kenet-el-Jalil (Jalil of course meaning Galilee). It is also known as Khirbet Kana, "the ruins of Kana." It is about five miles north of Kefr Kanna, eight and a half miles north of Nazareth. Being uninhabited ruins, the village is hard to find on any map, and no

Israeli tour buses stop at the site; all the traffic is to Kefr Kanna. At that town there is at least something to see and to buy. The ruins of Khirbet Kana are simply ruins, and largely unexcavated ones at that.

The name Kana translates as "place of reeds," and indeed there are many marshes at Khirbet Kana where reeds abound. Also the doubling of the "n" in Kanna makes it linguistically less likely that Kefr Kanna is the original Kana. Evidence for the authenticity of Khirbet Kana is confirmed by Josephus's statement in his first-century *Life* that he lived in the "village of Galilee named Cana," which he situates in "the plain of Asochis"—now identified with the Bet Netufa Valley where Khirbet Kana is situated. Early pilgrim tradition also points to Khirbet Kana as the site, since Theodosius writes in 530 that "it is five miles from Diocaesarea to Cana of Galilee." Before Diocaesarea changed its name in the time of Hadrian in the second century, it was known as Sepphoris—which is indeed five miles from Khirbet Kana. An anonymous pilgrim visiting the area in 570 reached much the same conclusion, saying that after he reached Diocaesarea/Sepphoris, "Three miles further on we reached Cana where the Lord attended a wedding."

At a minimum, one could say the claims of the now-ruined Kana are at least as strong as those of the commercially thriving Kanna. What seems to have decisively changed the direction of the pilgrim flow was the acquisition of property at Kefr Kanna by the Franciscans in 1641, when they bought a house near the local mosque. They succeeded in buying the mosque in 1879 and used the site to build their present church. Real evidence, therefore, for the authenticity of Kefr Kanna doesn't go back beyond the seventeenth century and is based largely on the similarity of names. For now, however, it will have to do, given the difficulty of getting to Khirbet Kana. Perhaps this can remain as a cautionary tale and a reminder that the authenticity of the biblical events does not depend upon the skill of archeologists—or the availability of package tours.

And ultimately the power of Cana's lesson does not depend upon locating the town today. Two thousand years ago, our Lord entered a humble village in the Galilean highlands and performed a completely unnecessary miracle for a completely obscure young couple. The miracle was unnecessary in that it did not concern great matters of life and death, like the cleansing of a leper or the raising of the dead. Certainly the infected leper who could not enter society and live among men, or the father of the girl who had just died, would have thought this miracle concerned a more trivial problem than theirs—namely, the disgrace that would befall a young couple when the wine ran out at their wedding. That would be memorably humiliating for them perhaps, but not life-destroying as are leprosy and death. They would get over it.

And the couple receiving the miracle were not important people: nothing is mentioned in the Gospel narrative about them or even their social importance. They have effectively vanished from the text, which simply relates, "There was a marriage in Cana of Galilee" (John 2:1). *And that is the point.* Jesus was not concerned only about the important people or about people with terrible and heartrending afflictions. He was concerned also about little people, and their little problems, and the little things of life. He came to bring joy to all the world, to low and high, to rich and poor together (Ps. 49:2). The social disgrace that would hang about a humble young couple concerned Him as much as the terrible afflictions of the great, just as His Father cared not only about the mighty men of the earth, but also about the humble sparrows that flew, so that not one of them was forgotten by Him (Luke 12:6).

When our Lord turned the water into wine so that the wedding party could continue as before, He revealed not only His glory (John 2:11) but also His tender condescension for all people everywhere, for the humble masses who would live and labor unnoticed and die in obscurity. They also were not forgotten by God. To them also He gives His joy and gladdens their heart. God not only looks upon those in mighty Rome, Jerusalem, Antioch, and Constantinople. He looks upon those in humble Cana as well.

Tabgha

By the sea is a grassy field with plenty of hay and many palm trees. By them are seven springs, each flowing strongly. And this is the field where the Lord fed the people with the five loaves and two fish. In fact the stone on which the Lord placed the bread has now been made into an altar. People who go there take away small pieces of the stone to bring them prosperity, and they are very effective. Past the walls of this church goes the public highway on which the apostle Matthew had his place of custom.

EGERIA, DESCRIBING
THE CHURCH AT TABGHA

Tabgha is a village on the edge of the Sea of Galilee. Its name is a corruption of the Greek *hepta pegon*, or "seven springs." There are indeed seven springs nearby. There is no archeological evidence of any settlements here in New Testament times, but it is a wonderful location—wonderful enough that from the fourth century churches were built here commemorating various events that occurred in our Lord's Galilean ministry. The Roman Catholic Church of the Multiplication is found here, a marvelous church preserving the original Byzantine structure that once stood in the spot, commemorating the miracle of the multiplication. Some of the mosaic floor from that period was even left. I looked at the portion of the mosaic floor and wondered if Egeria had walked upon it. A pamphlet available in the church describes it as the actual location where Christ multiplied the loaves in the wilderness. I have no doubt that in His travels throughout Galilee our Lord visited this lovely locale, and it served well to commemorate such things as the multiplication of the loaves. But as I looked down before me at the Sea of Galilee, the western side of which was ringed with towns in our Lord's day, I saw a problem.

The text of the Gospel says that our Lord, based in Capernaum, was so besieged with people needing His attention that "they did not even have time to eat" (Mark 6:31). To escape the crowds swarming through the area, "they departed to a deserted place in the boat by themselves" (v. 32)—that is, one far from the crowds. This was on the northeastern side of the lake: Luke 9:10 specifically identifies the town nearest to the site of the miracle as Bethsaida (that is, the new town of Bethsaida-Julias built at the top of the lake), and John 6:1 says Jesus "went over the Sea of Galilee" to perform the miracle, afterward crossing back westward to return to Capernaum (John 6:16–17).

So the text is clear that the site of the multiplication was a more or less uninhabited place near Bethsaida-Julias on the northeastern side of the lake. But Tabgha is on the western side. Admittedly the pamphlet from the church tries to offset this by suggesting, "While Matthew and Mark report two feedings [Matt. 14:13–21/Mark 6:30–44 and Matt. 15:32–39/Mark 8:1–10], Luke and John combine events into one. For them, the geographical frame (eastern shore) remains that of the second feeding, while the event reported is that of the first." In other words, Luke and John confused the two.

This is especially unlikely in the case of John, who is so precise with his facts that he often notes the time of day when something occurred (e.g. John 1:39; 4:6; 19:14). Besides, even apart from the unlikelihood of such confusion of accounts on the part of the apostles, Tabgha still could not remotely be considered an *eremos topos*, a deserted place. It was located on the lakeside, and Capernaum itself was a mile and a half away. It is hard to imagine how walking a mile or so down the road to another lakeside town could conceivably be described as "depart[ing] from there by boat to a deserted place" by themselves (Matt. 14:13). And why would they need a boat? It was just down the road. The boat would indeed be needed to cross to Bethsaida-Julias, but not to hike next door to the site of modern Tabgha.

We never did travel to the site of Bethsaida-Julias, given time constraints, but we enjoyed seeing Tabgha nonetheless. From the days of Egeria, Christians had come here to look upon the serenity that is the sea of Galilee and upon its gently rolling hills, and to return in spirit to the time when Christ walked those hills and preached to the multitudes. The exact hill from which our Lord preached the Sermon on the Mount (Matt. 5:1) cannot perhaps be known with certainty, but from Tabgha, we could see many likely candidates.

Here was a place where one could feast—if not upon bread and fishes, then at least upon the timeless words of the Lord.

From the days of Egeria, Christians have come here and found in the seven springs a place of rest. As I looked around at the rolling hills, I felt a tremendous peace and could well understand why earlier Christians had built their church here. I would gladly have stayed for many hours at Tabgha.

Kursi

The ruins of Kursi are known for being the place where the Lord once healed the demoniac (as narrated in Matt. 8:28–34; Mark 5:1–10; Luke 8:26–31). It is around "the other side" of the lake from Capernaum, the eastern side, in ancient Gaulanitis (technically distinct from Galilee). Much of the Decapolis was there (compare Mark 5:20)—a collection of ten cities (hence the name Decapolis, which means "ten cities") that were centers of Greek and Roman culture in an otherwise Semitic world.

The story is well known. When Christ and His disciples emerged on the eastern shore of the Sea of Galilee, a demoniac met them, raging and crying out. At length Christ cast out a legion of demons from the poor wretch and restored the man to sanity. Before the demons were cast out, however, they begged Christ not to send them into the abyss, but to allow them to enter the nearby herd of swine. Christ allowed this, and they came out without further hurting the man (compare Mark 9:26 for a possible fate for the man if the demons had not been allowed to leave quietly). The demons entered the swine, which immediately went berserk, stampeded over the edge of the steep bank where they were feeding, and perished in the sea beneath the cliff.

The historical challenge has been to identify which town is the town mentioned in the New Testament account. Matthew places the story "in the country of the Gadarenes" (Matt. 8:28), but he cannot mean us to regard Gadara as the nearby town, for Gadara, though the head city of the region, is six miles from the lakeshore. By the phrase "the country of the Gadarenes" Matthew simply means the area in the region around Gadara—that is, the eastern side of the lake. Mark and Luke both present different readings, according to which manuscript is used. One reading has "the country of the Gerasenes"; another has "the country of the Gergesenes." The problem with the former reading is that the town of Gerasa is some thirty miles southeast of the lake. The latter reading, indicating the town of Gergesa, alone fits the bill, being on the lake, with cliffs nearby, and having caves for tombs close at hand (compare Mark 5:5). The site is now known as Kursi. It is no longer a town but a national park.

We reached it easily enough, and after paying the entry fee, stepped back in time. We climbed up the steep hill to the ruins of a small chapel, marking the place where the pigs stampeded downhill to their death. The ruins included a Byzantine mosaic floor and some columns. I could imagine the Christians of an earlier time sitting here and looking down upon the same waters of the lake that I saw. And as we looked up at the hill stretching above us, we could easily imagine a large herd of swine stampeding down from its fatal height.

We descended the hill to visit the even more fascinating excavations below, surely the prize of the area. We soon found ourselves walking through the ruins of a well-preserved Byzantine church, which included a baptistery. The presence of a baptistery witnessed to the presence of a once-thriving Christian community.

I stood amid the stones and wandered around and around the ruined church. I could discern how things must have looked in centuries past—where the narthex was, where the nave, where the altar, where the baptistery. We could find the remnants of the *synthronon*—the semicircular bench to the east of the altar in the apse that served as seats for the bishop and his clergy. I took my (very belated) seat there, taking care not to sit in the bishop's place, so that my diaconal friend could take my picture. As I wandered over the ruins, I could almost see the congregation milling about, praying, listening to their bishop as he preached from his place at the *synthronon*. The place felt happily haunted by the spirits of brothers in Christ long gone. I wondered about their names, and what it felt like to worship there, and for how long the bishop preached.

The church in Gergesa was probably built in the fifth century, and it continued, surviving Persian invasion and later fires. During its day, Christian pilgrims came from all over to see the place where Christ liberated the demoniac by the shores of the sea. Such pilgrims stopped coming in about the ninth century, as Islam took its inevitable toll in the Holy Land, and things dried up. Whatever community grew up around the church has also gone, leaving only greenery. When the excavators dug through the earth in the nearby chapel, they found the skeletons of thirty men, probably some of the clergy who once walked in the church and sat on the *synthronon*. Gergesa and its bishop and its Christians have vanished; now only lonely Kursi remains.

Capernaum

> *In Capernaum the house of the prince of the apostles has been made into a church, with its original walls still standing. It is where the Lord healed the paralytic. There also is the synagogue where the Lord cured a man possessed by the devil. The way in is up many stairs, and it is made of dressed stone.*
>
> EGERIA, DESCRIBING THE CHURCH
> AND SYNAGOGUE IN CAPERNAUM

Perhaps the most interesting stop in our breathless race around the lake was Capernaum (from the Hebrew *kefr-nahum* or "village of Nahum," doubtless the original settler on the site). In our Lord's day it was a larger town than Nazareth, numbering several thousand people. Many of course would have been fishermen, but Capernaum was also a trade station, linked by roads to other important cities. It was therefore a place of commerce and quite wealthy. Of course, as a border town, it had a customs house (or tax office) as well (Mark 2:13–14). Nazareth, where Jesus was born, may have preserved a rustic simplicity, but Capernaum, where He made His new residence and base, was a thriving town with its face set toward the wide world.

There is nothing there now, apart from the preserved ruins of synagogue and church. After the Persians swept through Palestine in the seventh century and carried all before them in a flood of destruction and bloodshed, the northern town never recovered. By the thirteenth century, a pilgrim visiting there reported that it was "just despicable; it numbers only seven houses of poor fishermen." But in its Byzantine day, when the largess of the emperor was filling the world with churches and monasteries, Capernaum got its fair share.

From the earliest days, of course, Christians looked upon the town as their original home, the seed from which they grew, the womb from which they emerged. They knew which house Peter lived in and continued to regard it with devotion. From the first days, it was a house where the Christians would meet for worship, and Capernaum itself became something of a hotbed of Christian discipleship. No doubt the disciples lived somewhat uneasily next to their non-Christian Jewish neighbors—Peter's house, which served as the Christian headquarters, was just eighty-four feet from the local synagogue.

That house, now excavated beneath the ruins of the later

church, indeed has been dated to the first century. It was larger than most other houses in the area, with coarse walls and a roof of earth and straw (compare Mark 2:4), and consisted of a few rooms around two open courtyards. The excavations discovered coins, oil lamps, and fishhooks (!) that date to the first century. They also show that the large central room was plastered from ceiling to floor—unusual for poor houses in that time and only done in places put to public use. In an earlier excavated layer, one found pottery cooking pots and eating bowls, whereas the excavation of a later layer revealed storage containers and oil lamps. In other words, from about the mid-first century, the building was decisively changed from a house that was also used for worship to a place used for worship alone.

In the fourth century, walls were added to surround the house, each wall about eighty-eight feet long, and a roof was installed. The place then looked more like a church and less like a house, and Egeria, visiting it later that century, wrote, "In Capernaum the house of the prince of the apostles has been made into a church, though with its original walls left standing."

In the fifth century, the building was renovated still further as the local church grew in prestige. An octagonal basilica and baptistery were built over it, preserving the original structure beneath. Thus it remained until the Persians came and everything that was in their way went down in flames.

There is a beautiful Roman Catholic church now built over the top of the house. In the nave is a glass floor, so that one can look down and see the original house of Peter below. As with most things Franciscan in the Holy Land, the rule is "Look, but don't touch": we can peer below but not enter the site itself. From outside and from within the modern church I looked into the ruins, imagining Peter living there and our Lord using his house as His base in Capernaum. Somewhere down there, just a few yards away, it all happened. But all signs of human habitation had gone, leaving just the bare rock.

I took the inevitable photographs, trying to capture the place from every angle. The worst was trying to photograph the original site through the Franciscan glass from the church above. For me any spiritual connection was utterly lost, submerged in tourism. I felt as if a living connection had been killed and unnaturally preserved behind the glass, like a dead butterfly pinned to a board.

But every day has its blessings and every disappointment its consolation. As I wandered about the edges of the ruins outside, I saw a cat, which jumped up to where I was lingering and asked me to scratch its head for a while. We shared the moment as we both paused by the house of Peter, I scratching the cat's head and it purring with contentment. I had my diaconal friend take a photo of the two of us together.

Right next to the excavations of Peter's house were the excavated ruins of the synagogue. Archeologists could identify two phases of building: the original synagogue dating from the first century (using the usual black basalt stones common in the area) and the later synagogue built above it in about the fourth or fifth century, using large white stones brought from elsewhere. The synagogue is one of the largest in Palestine and must have exuded a sense of grandeur. Much of it remains, and one can easily distinguish the black stones of the original structure (now part of the foundation) from the later white ones.

Given that Christians and Jews continued to live together in Capernaum into the fifth century and beyond, I could not help but wonder about the relations between them. Capernaum, while not exactly a backwater, was still a town in the Galilean highland, not a vast metropolis like Rome or Alexandria. Two rival groups could coexist in those large cities and find ways not to get in each other's way. It must have been much more difficult in Capernaum, and all the more so since the grandly built synagogue and the imperially endowed church stood only eighty-four feet apart.

Surely some competition must have raged between them, especially since their views concerning Jesus were incompatible with one another. For those worshipping in the synagogue and directing their prayers southward to Jerusalem, Jesus, though hailed by the world in the fourth and fifth centuries as the divine Son of God whose followers were now ascendant in the empire, was still a blasphemer and a deceiver, and it was customary to add the phrase "may his name perish" whenever it was mentioned. For those worshipping just next door in the church and directing their prayers eastward, Jesus was God in the flesh, the One to whom they all had given their lives.

One wonders if the space between the two structures was not something of a no-man's-land. Certainly the desire of the Jewish population to enlarge their synagogue to such lofty proportions must have had something to do with their defiant response to the then-ascendant Christian Faith. They must have felt themselves locked in battle for the souls of men and the heart of Capernaum.

Time has swept them all away now. We Christians are no longer ascendant in the world, and our splendid octagonal basilica in Capernaum lies in ruins, the object of excavators. Peter's house no longer rings with the praises of his Lord but now sleeps its long sleep, safely below Franciscan glass. But the faith of Peter remains, and we who share it may delight to return to our very first home and look longingly at the remains of an early springtime long ago.

As I wandered the ruins of the synagogue site in which our Lord preached, and gazed into the first structure that ever housed His disciples, the veil of the centuries seemed to wear very thin indeed. I wondered where within these few yards He had stood when He worshipped in that synagogue and cast out a demon from a possessed man (Mark 1:21–28).

Before we left Capernaum, we climbed down to the lakeside and sat on its stones, gazing out at the Sea of Galilee. It was utterly serene and seemingly eternal. It had seen the waxing and waning of empires and had changed its name over and over again—from the Sea of Chinnereth (i.e. "the harp," for its harplike shape), to the Sea of Genneseret (according to some, a Hellenized form of Chinnereth), to the Sea of Galilee, to the Sea of Tiberias. Despite these changes, it endured and always returned to peace.

We sat there for a long time, soaking in its peace, dipping our bare feet and washing our faces in its waters. Somewhere Palestinians were suffering and weeping, and across a nearby border Syrians were killing each other in a hopeless bloodbath, but here it all seemed far away. The Sea of Galilee had seen conflicts of all kinds come and go, both the close-quartered hostility of Christian and Jew in Capernaum and the many invading armies that seemed never to cease troubling this land.

Sitting beside the lake, we looked out on a view that had scarcely changed since the days when Christ looked out at it and St. Peter fished its waters. It seemed to bid us take the long view. One day, all these wars would cease and the quarrelers fall silent, even as the Jews and Christians who worshipped eighty-four feet from one another in the fifth century one day fell silent. What ultimately matters, both in Galilee and elsewhere, are the things that are eternal.

We walked back to the taxi a little quieter than we had come. Once again I wished I could have lingered longer in the peace that was Galilee.

~: 8 :~

Recovering The Via Dolorosa

In returning to Jerusalem after our visit to Galilee, I wanted to visit the so-called Tower of David, or the Citadel, located toward the southwest corner of the Old City. It contains an excellent museum offering a tour of its premises, including access to its summit, which itself affords a splendid view of the Old City. The exhibits inside contain maps and diagrams showing how the city grew from the time of David, adding the Temple grounds northward in the reign of Solomon and expanding westward in the reign of Hezekiah. It was enthralling and well worth the entrance fee. But I was looking for something not found in the provided tour. I was looking for the shadow of Pilate. For it was somewhere here or nearby that Herod had his palace, and according to some scholars, it was this palace that Pilate used for his residence, or praetorium, when he stayed in Jerusalem.

All questions involving the route of our Lord from condemnation to execution—the so-called *Via Dolorosa* or "way of sorrows"—must begin with this question. We know where the route ended—at the place now called the Church of the Holy Sepulcher, which in our Lord's time was just outside the city gates. (The claims of Gordon's Calvary or the Garden Tomb north of the present Old City walls are scarcely worth refuting and have long since been refuted by scholars. Like the Protestantism of his day, Gordon despised the Catholic/Byzantine church and ignored its history. In 1883 he wanted to find a site unspoiled by history and found it north of the present city walls. His theological justification for the site's authenticity now reads like science fiction.)

So, since we know the terminus of the route, the only real question is, "Where did it begin?" The Gospels all insist that it began with Christ's condemnation by Pilate at "the praetorium." But where was this?

Since the Middle Ages, the location of the praetorium was thought to be the Antonia Tower in the northwest corner of the Temple area, the barracks for the Roman garrison guarding Jerusalem. This was next to the Temple, since the Romans wanted to keep close watch on the Temple grounds and be able to respond quickly should a riot erupt there. (St. Paul had reason to be thankful for such proximity; read Acts 21:30–32.) This is the site presupposed by those accepting the authenticity of the present Via Dolorosa, which traces a route from the Antonia Tower to the Church of the Holy Sepulcher. But acceptance of this route and its use for liturgical procession dates only from the thirteenth century. Indeed, the Byzantine topography of the city did not accept the Antonia Tower as the site of the praetorium, but St. Sophia's church, located elsewhere to the south. There is no continuous tradition tracing this route as the true one. It is a possible route, but other routes may be considered as well.

There are problems with thinking that Pilate used the Antonia Tower as his praetorium when in Jerusalem. Firstly, St. Matthew informs us that Pilate's wife was with him (Matt. 27:19), and it is unlikely that Pilate would have taken soldiers' quarters in the barracks in the rough Antonia Tower under those circumstances. Josephus admittedly describes it as "having the largeness and form of a palace" (*Wars* 5, 5, 8), but it is likely that by this he means only "the largeness and form of a palace compared to other barracks for soldiers." One wonders if Pilate's wife would have found it so palatial.

Moreover, Josephus refers to "the royal palace" in the Upper City (*Wars* 2, 19,4). By this he referred to Herod's palace, which contained three towers, named after Herod's family and friends: the tower Phasael (after Herod's brother), and the towers Hippicus (after Herod's general) and Mariamne (after Herod's wife). The present so-called Tower of David is the remnants of the only one of those towers remaining, the tower Phasael (though some suggest it is the Hippicus tower). In other words, Herod's royal palace was located at the place now occupied by the Tower of David.

But was it used by Pilate as his praetorium while he stayed in Jerusalem? The available evidence points in that direction. Philo (d. AD 50) writes in his *Delegation to Gaius* that Herod's palace in the Holy City was "the residence of the prefects," and according to Josephus the prefect Gessius Florus resided "in the palace" from AD 64 (*Wars* 2, 14, 8). Thus when ancient readers read that "the soldiers led Him away into the hall called Praetorium" (Mark 15:16), they would have understood by this term the palace of Herod.

So the Crusader route is probably not the correct one. The true Via Dolorosa began at the royal palace, the praetorium, someplace in or near the Tower of David (for the praetorium covered more area than does the present tower, which is all that is left of it). The normal route would have involved going from the praetorium by way of what is now St. James Street to the main north-south road, the present Chabad Street. (This road was rebuilt after the city was razed in about 135, and then renamed as the Roman *Cardo Maximus*.) This north-south road was the artery closest to the praetorium and led northward out of the city through what was then known to Josephus as the Gennath Gate (or "garden gate") because there was then a garden outside the gate.

The location of this gate is where the current David Street meets with the bazaars. The "garden" for which the gate was named was of course the garden containing some tombs, including the one belonging to Joseph of Arimathea. The little crag not far from it was just outside the city; it was evidently the usual place where the Romans executed criminals. This was Golgotha, with Joseph's tomb nearby. This was the true Via Dolorosa; it was by this sorrowful way that Christ accomplished His exodus at Jerusalem (Luke 9:31).

This means, of course, that the Via Dolorosa appearing on the street signs and explained patiently by the guides is incorrect; the true one was a northward route to the Church of the Holy Sepulcher from the Palace of Herod, not a westward one from the Antonia Tower. And by any figuring it was lower than the route shown today, since the Jerusalem Christ knew was between ten and twenty feet further down than the present city (ancient cities tended to be built on top of themselves; hence the ability of archeologists to date their finds). This is particularly damaging to the claims made by the various Stations of the Cross scattered throughout the Old City, all of which assume the medieval Crusader route.

Thus the Church of the Condemnation, for example, originally a Byzantine church and now in Franciscan hands, cannot be the place where Christ was condemned. The Church of the Flagellation, wonderful though its 1920s architecture and stained glass may be, cannot be the place where He was flagellated. And the Ecce Homo Basilica, though the Franciscans there delight in showing an excavated paved gaming floor where they said the Roman soldiers played at dice before they mocked Christ, cannot actually be the place where those soldiers heard Pilate utter the words "*Ecce homo*" ("Behold the man!" John 19:5).

Indeed, here the Franciscans are doubly wrong, for not only does the true route not support the Ecce Homo site, but the building itself has since been dated to the time of Hadrian, who rebuilt the city around 135. The Ecce Homo arch was a part of that rebuilding; Pilate never saw it. The Polish Catholic church that marks the site of Christ's first fall must forfeit that claim, despite having an elegant sculpture of it, as must the unfortunately named Armenian Church of our Lady of the Spasm, which marks the place where Christ met His Mother.

The claim of the small Franciscan church to be the place where Christ encountered Simon of Cyrene also has no credibility. And even less credibility attaches to their claim that the discolored stone on the right side of the building is discolored because Christ leaned against it while Simon assisted Him. As my traveling companion instantly realized, this stone could not be authentic because, whatever the true route of the Via Dolorosa, the original road by which Christ traveled now lies many feet below the present level of the city.

The place where St. Veronica wiped Christ's face so that the cloth miraculously retained its imprint is marked by a Greek Catholic chapel appropriately called the Holy Face. Orthodox may be particularly interested in this chapel, because although there was no St. Veronica who wiped the Lord's face (the word *veronica* is a corruption of the words *vera icon*, "true image"), the chapel does hold some Orthodox icons of the Holy Face. For many Orthodox this Face refers to our Lord's miraculous image imprinted on the Holy Shroud, usually known as the Shroud of Turin. The image on that, some say, was imprinted not by a woman wiping His face as He went to His Cross, but by the Lord alone as He rose from the dead at His Resurrection. Yet whatever the authenticity of the Shroud of Turin, the authenticity of the station of the Holy Face chapel cannot be sustained, since our Lord did not walk to Golgotha by that route.

The same must be said of the other stations where Christ fell the second and third times, or where He spoke to the grieving women of Jerusalem. In fact it is only when it reaches the area surrounding the Church of the Holy Sepulcher that the supposed Via Dolorosa intersects and combines with the real one.

For those to whom historical accuracy or even probability matters, it is important to remember that the events occurring on the way to the Cross were the creation of the medieval West, and none can claim any real historicity. That Christ was condemned is certain, and probably also that He fell at least once, since Simon was seized upon by the Roman soldiers to help Christ carry the crossbeam (Mark 15:21). He is also recorded as speaking to the women of Jerusalem (Luke 23:28–31), though the location of the exchange is not stated or known. The other elements are the product of medieval fancy.

Other sites presented to the piety of pilgrims conflict with each other even more. Particularly puzzling in this respect is the Prison of Christ. Some Orthodox claim that the prison in which Christ was held before His death is found beneath a Greek Orthodox monastery church near the Ecce Homo arch and the Hospice Junction. One descends a forbidding series of steps from the Greek Orthodox Praetorium to some underground caves, one of which is pointed out as the Prison of Christ. A rock bench with two holes in it is displayed (with the obliging visual aid of an icon) as the place where Christ was confined, His legs placed through those holes in the rock. My companion was, I think, of warmer piety than I. He could find something there, but I was appalled by its lack of historicity and desperate attempt to grab some of the tourist trade, and I couldn't leave quickly enough. I took no photographs.

But there is a place within the Church of the Holy Sepulcher that also claims to be the Holy Prison in which Christ was held. It can be found on the northeast side of the main catholicon. There is a carved image of the double-headed Byzantine eagle in the floor in front of the chapel, and within is an altar, below which are two round holes in the floor, ostensibly made by the feet of Jesus. This is odd, since the holes are large and completely round, and not in any way shaped like footprints.

There is another claim, that of the Armenians, who believe

that a recess in the Monastery of the Flagellation is the authentic prison. Yet another claimant is one of the caves beneath the Church of St. Peter in Gallicantu in the far south of the city, believed to be the home of the high priest. Presumably it formed Christ's prison in the time before He was handed over to Pilate. The grottos in St. Peter's are indeed very deep, though it was not unusual for houses in that era to have such caves, which served as cellars and cisterns.

All of these claimants to be the authentic prison of Christ constitute an embarrassment of riches, for obviously not all of the claims can be correct. It appears that any church that possessed a grotto anywhere along the presumed Via Dolorosa or even near it put forward the claim, displaying whatever artifact or rocklike oddity they possessed as evidence. Yet one wants to find the actual place, if it exists. It is disappointing to think that the place where Christ was detained and questioned by Pilate no longer exists as such, and that no one can point to a room or cave and say, "This was the place."

I suggest something altogether different—that Christ's trial was over so quickly that He probably wasn't held in a deep prison at all. For think of it: at His predawn trial before the Sanhedrin, after He was hustled in to see Annas for a quick interview and high-priestly fishing expedition to collect evidence against Him (John 18:19–24), His presence was needed before the Sanhedrin all night long as they vainly sought for testimony against Him. They would not have wasted valuable time keeping Him in a deep grotto in the basement of the house of the high priest. After a midnight arrest, they had only until dawn to secure the needed condemnation—one they only got at the last minute when He "incriminated" Himself by confessing to be the Christ (Matt. 26:63–66). There was no time or reason to waste valuable minutes by imprisoning Him in a hole.

It was the same at His Roman trial before Pilate. This trial began when the courts opened at dawn, and according to Mark, by mid-morning or so He was already hanging on the Cross (Mark 15:25). Even if one takes Mark's "third hour" (9:00 AM) to mean loosely "early in the day" and accepts the Johannine chronology as more exact, so that Pilate was condemning Him as the sixth hour (noon) drew near, that still allowed no time for incarceration. According to the Gospel narrative, Christ was hauled before Pilate at dawn, examined by him, sent off to Herod for examination, mocked by Herod, returned to Pilate, reexamined by Pilate, sent for scourging, brought out to the people, disowned by them in favor of Barabbas at a public meeting, and then finally sentenced by Pilate to be crucified. He then was brought to the place at the praetorium where He picked up His Cross and staggered out with it to the place of death and execution outside the city gates—and all before noon, or possibly by 9:00 AM.

When in all this activity would there have been time to hold Him in prison? And why would anyone have done that? His presence was urgently required by the Sanhedrin and by Pilate so that He could stand trial and answer questions. It served no one's purpose to imprison Him anywhere. The Jews did not want Him imprisoned, but killed. Pilate did not want Him imprisoned, but tried swiftly and out of his way. Once again, there was neither reason nor time to imprison Jesus at all from the time He first appeared before Pilate to the time He was nailed to the Cross.

A revised understanding of the Via Dolorosa means, of course, that many of the Christian sites in the Old City should properly stand down from much of their boasting. The Church of the Flagellation, for example, can offer nothing more than other churches can offer—a quiet place to pray and find the presence of Christ. That is still worthwhile, but one doesn't need to travel to Jerusalem to find it; it can be found at the church around the corner back home. Accepting a revised Via Dolorosa would reconfigure the spiritual map of the Old City, a map that has been relied upon since the Crusades—and would possibly kill much of the tourist trade there, since many of the churches in the Old City would at a stroke be stripped of their biblical significance.

Walking a revised Via Dolorosa would bring one from the area along the Tower of David along James Street to the Chabad and north on David Street to the Holy Sepulcher. There would be no church sites along that way to inspire or pray in, no suggestion as to where along that way Christ fell (if indeed He did) or where He spoke to the grieving women. It would be a quiet and perhaps solitary walk, with not much to nourish a devotionally hungry heart. Perhaps for this reason alone, it seems that the traditional route is in no danger of being supplanted by another route better favored by history and archeology.

Does that mean that walking the traditional Via Dolorosa has no value? Not at all. For the true value of walking that route—either the traditional Crusader route or the more probable one—is not found in geographical accuracy. What matters more is the geography of the heart and the devotion poured out by the believer along the way. Walking the Via Dolorosa has always been more than a merely historical exercise. It has been a devotional journey, an attempt to relive the final hours of Christ with Him, to try to bring home to the normally all-too-cold human heart some of the pathos and power of the death of Christ. One walks and prays, and stops and reads and prays, and walks and prays some more. It is the prayer that counts, not the steps. The fruit of the journey consists not in the accuracy of the route, but in the outpourings of love for the Lord, who loved us enough to walk a way of sorrows to save us. That is why, in Roman Catholic churches in the West, each church once contained the Stations of the Cross, offering the fruit of the Via Dolorosa to those who would never be able to go to Jerusalem.

We need to worship God with the mind and not uncritically accept everything a guide tells us. But the head must not be separated from the heart, for it is with the heart that we choose to love God; it is with the heart that man believes (Rom. 10:10). I would never disparage the Via Dolorosa. Indeed, I think it precious enough to refine, correct, and bathe in historical truth.

I therefore all the more wanted to see the place where Christ had His last interviews with Pilate and where He was finally condemned. My prowling about the museum and ramparts of the Tower of David brought few echoes of Pilate's praetorium, but then I did not expect it to. The original royal palace had covered both the Tower of David and other area as well, and it had been effectively demolished long ago by the Romans, who left only these fragments. The museum had other concerns than mine, and there was no way of knowing precisely where the palace began and ended, nor what it would've looked like, though we can be sure that Herod built it to a grand scale and made it as sumptuous as possible. That was the way he did things, bringing luxury even to his palace in the windy wilderness, in Masada.

There was little for my hungry historical imagination to feed on, apart from the conclusion that somewhere within a block or so from here, Pilate paced up and down, rubbed his eyes in frustration over the political and judicial problem the Sanhedrin had handed him, and at length washed his hands of it all. Somewhere within a block or so, Christ stood silent before His accusers like a lamb led to slaughter; somewhere not too far away, His back was laid open by scourges, and they laid the crossbeam upon Him. Somewhere close to where I stood in the sunlight near the present Tower of David, Christ staggered northward to the beckoning city gate, carrying His Cross and the sins of us all.

The day was drawing to a close when I left the Tower of David. I made the sign of the cross and walked out into the setting sun.

~: 9 :~

The Temple and Its Area

The Wailing Wall

On Sunday we went to the Temple—or rather to the Temple Mount—and the area surrounding it. After our usual visit to the Church of the Holy Sepulcher (it was Sunday, after all), we walked to the entrance to the Temple Mount and passed through the expected metal detectors and the expected cold suspicion and hostility of those operating them. Soon we were facing all that was left of the Temple after the Romans were finished with it—namely, the Western Wall, popularly known as the Wailing Wall.

Even in its desolation, it was still remarkable and a testimony to the ambitious greatness of Herod, who filled his land with such buildings. Since we were not Jews, my companion and I were not allowed to approach the wall that day, despite a nearby sign boasting, with perhaps unintended irony, in the prophetic words of Isaiah 56:7 that "My House shall be called a house of prayer for all peoples." We didn't spend much time there, since we were not allowed to approach the wall to offer our own prayers. All that was left was to photograph the devotion of others and that tall, formidable wall, which stood like a lonely, defiant fragment of a now-dead past.

Many Jews were standing at the wall itself and praying, some casually, some with great fervency, and some with the swaying back and forth that had become customary of such Jewish prayer since at least medieval times. According to pious Jewish thought, God has never ceased to watch over His Temple, and His Presence has never been withdrawn from it, even after its destruction in AD 70. This doubtless accounted for the constant crowd of the Jewish faithful at the wall. For them the wall is not simply a remnant of a former glory, a holy relic made of stone. For them, God still dwells in this place as He did when the Temple stood tall in the morning sun and its unbroken shimmering white stones reflected its rays. For them, the Romans reducing all to rubble changed nothing. That is why they still come to its sacred wall. That is why they refuse to tread on the Temple Mount, for fear of trespassing upon the Holy of Holies.

Their famous perseverance at their wall and their fear of

violating sacred space throws into high relief a difference between the Old Covenant and the New: the concept of *temple*. Ancient Mosaic religion, like all ancient religions, built a shrine for God, a place set apart that could act as a nexus between heaven and earth, between God and men. In ancient religious thought, that place might be anywhere. It might be a sacred oak or grove, it might be a high place of earth, it might be a little homemade hut containing the image of the deity. It might, if God so willed, be a burning bush, one that burned yet was not consumed. It might be a large and adorned temple made of fitted stones and lined with cedar.

But in all cases, it was a place apart, a place that was holy, separated, a place where men removed their sandals and trod with fear. For it was in this place that man met with the unseen, with the deity, and supplicated divine favor through sacrifice. That is why the loss of the sacrificial altar was so catastrophic at the Babylonian captivity (compare the Song of the Three Young Men, v. 15: "at this time there is no place to make an offering before You or to find mercy").

Those more familiar with the Bible than with world history might imagine that the Temple built by Solomon was unique in the world of his day. In fact, Solomon's Temple was simply the Hebrew version of something that existed the world over. It was a house where God dwelt, and the altar outside smoked continually with the carcasses of animals offered in sacrifice, the food that He ate. The Hebrews thus sought the favor of

Yahweh, even as the Moabites sought the favor of Chemosh, and the Ammonites sought the favor of Moloch. Other nations had their own deities who resided in their own temples and were fed and supplicated at their own altars.

There were of course many differences between the religion of Yahweh and those of the other deities, such as a commitment to the sole monotheistic power of Yahweh, as well as the assertion that He did not need those sacrifices as men needed their food. But these differences ought not to blind us to the basic similarities between all ancient religions. All religions said their deities dwelt in their temples. Yahweh's temple was in Zion; He dwelt in Jerusalem (Ps. 135:21). One could offer prayer from anywhere, but to worship Him, one needed to come to where He was: "Three times in the year all your males shall appear before the Lord God" (Ex. 23:17).

Admittedly the prophetic voices in Israel at that time did their best to refine the concept so that people would not think their God was somehow confined to His Temple. He was bigger than that. Solomon dedicated the Temple with the words, "Will God indeed dwell on the earth? Behold, heaven and the heaven of heavens cannot contain You. How much less this temple which I have built!" (1 Kings 8:27). Isaiah prophesied, "Thus says the Lord: 'Heaven is My throne, / And earth is My footstool. / Where is the house that you will build Me?'" (Is. 66:1).

But these prophetic cautions did not overthrow the basic principle in all religion that a deity chose a location on the earth and made it holy. For all the differences between the religion of Moses and the religion of the pagans (and these differences are many and profound), they share this in common: they both confess that God chooses a place. Biblical Mosaic religion was emphatic that God's Presence was not pledged to the place unconditionally. He would remove His Presence if the people sinned (see Ezek. 10:1–22 for a description of this removal prior to the Babylonian captivity). But the norm was that God had a spatially localized Presence.

This bit of ancient religion was transcended in Christ, along with many other bits (bits like the concept of clean and unclean food; compare Mark 7:19). God no longer needs a temple to manifest His Presence, whether the temple be on Mount Gerizim or in Jerusalem (John 4:21). Men no longer need temples, or altars, or priesthoods (that is, others set aside in a state of ritual purity to pour out the blood of sacrifice upon the altars). Old Covenant religion has now been recapitulated and embodied in Christ. He is now the true temple. He is now the true priest. He is the sacrifice and the altar.

Since Christ's ascension into heaven and sitting at the right hand of the Father, the true locus of all authentic worship is in heaven. That is why we worship "in the heavenly *places*" (Eph. 1:3), for that is where the true and saving sacrifice is offered and received. By the Spirit we lift up our hearts and find ourselves spiritually no longer earthbound but in heaven. By the Spirit, we Christians can access the heavenly worship and sacrifice wherever we gather, whether we gather in Jerusalem, or Samaria, or even to the ends of the earth (Acts 1:8). Now wherever His disciples meet in eucharistic assembly, Christ is present among them in saving sacramental power. Our buildings may come and go—and in the Holy Land I looked upon the ruins of many that have gone—but our sacrificial access to God remains the same.

Our zeal to find the holy places of past worship has nothing whatsoever to do with mourning a past glory, much less with lamenting the loss of an altar that gave access to God. We do not stand and mourn and pray and rock back and forth, lamenting an altar now gone. We still have an altar, wherever we may be, and no earthly army can take it from us (Heb. 13:10). We have a temple, once torn down by men, but now raised up and imperishable (John 2:19). Let others stand and wail. Those who know Christ have done with such sorrow forever.

The Dome of The Rock

After this we entered the broad open courts containing the Dome of the Rock and the al-Aqsa Mosque, the former of which is possibly the most famous building in Jerusalem. The Dome of the Rock is the third holiest shrine in Islam. It commemorates Muhammad's Night Journey, when according to Islam he took a miraculous journey through the seven heavens, meeting in turn the prophets Moses, Aaron, Jesus, and others. The journey, taken on a winged supernatural horse, began from these courts.

This Islamic shrine stands on the site of the original Temple that Herod built and the Romans destroyed in AD 70. The Christians, when culturally ascendant in the fourth century, did not clean up the Roman rubble but left it as a perpetual witness that our Lord's words predicting the destruction of the Temple had been fulfilled.

When the Muslims conquered Jerusalem in the seventh century, they eventually decided to use the Temple site to build a splendid structure of their own. They were concerned, the stories say, that the splendor of the Church of the Holy Sepulcher (then called "the Church of the Resurrection") might lure Muslims away from Islam to Christianity. They therefore decided to build a glorious structure as a statement of the superiority of Islam. The polemical intent of the project is apparent even today—the verses chosen to adorn the interior of the Dome of the Rock are the anti-Christian ones: "God has no companion," "It is not fitting to God that He should beget a son," and "In the name of the one God pray for your prophet and servant, Jesus son of Mary."

As my companion and I began removing our shoes in preparation to enter the mosque, we were told quite plainly that only Muslims could enter. I was tempted to comment on how the Muslim exclusivity about their Dome mirrored perfectly the Jewish exclusivity about their Wall, but thought better of it. We therefore walked about, admiring the beautiful exteriors and taking photographs. The Dome of the Rock is quite small compared with the original Temple, and it contains only about half as much bulk. As we walked about the courtyard, we could imagine a little of what visitors to the Temple must have felt like, since the Temple was also set amid a large courtyard, the Court of the Gentiles. It was those courts that helped connect me with the biblical past, not the buildings set within them. Once again I felt that geography was my friend, even if architecture was not. The buildings such as the Temple had all gone, but the patch of earth on which they once stood remained.

The historical association of Jerusalem and the Dome of the Rock with Mohammad is rather ephemeral, to say the least. Examining the historical background to Mohammad's fabled Night Journey leads one back to an earlier time when he was just consolidating his strength. Though he had never visited Jerusalem himself (his followers would not conquer and march into the city until two years after his death), he was still claiming to be a true prophet and one who was superior to all the other Jewish prophets that came before him. Many of his followers began to doubt his authority, and he needed something to shore it up.

He therefore claimed to have visited Jerusalem during a single night journey, led by the angel Gabriel. Gabriel, he said, led him to a white mule with wings at its thighs. Mohammad mounted the spirit beast, and it carried him into the sky. He arrived at Jerusalem, where he met Abraham, Moses, and Jesus.

They asked him to lead them in prayer, which he did. He then ascended the steed and was carried up through the seven heavens, being shown many revelations, and was given instructions on prayer by God for the faithful Muslims. He then returned to the earth, where his disappearance apparently had not been noted. If all the prophets of old acknowledged him as a prophet, he told his followers, surely they could too.

The story reminded me of similar tales in Mormonism, such as Joseph Smith's claim to have met the angel Moroni, who told him where golden plates written in Reformed Egyptian were buried, and how the magic eyeglasses buried with them could enable him to translate them into the *Book of Mormon*.

Here I will only observe that apart from Mohammad's story of his Night Journey, Islam has no connection with Jerusalem other than its age-old military conquest of the city. Therefore the Dome of the Rock cannot possess the same historical significance for Muslims that it does for Christians and Jews, much of whose sacred history is bound up with the physical place. The Dome of the Rock, for all its beauty, is basically just a building that shields its worshippers from the elements, in which they can come and offer prayer. I walked around admiring the beauty of the buildings, becoming certain that for Islam the inner and original significance of these courts was simply as an assertion of cultural supremacy, with Islamic architecture triumphing over Christian. Islam owned the streets (or at least these courts), and that was the true source of attachment to this place.

As I left those gorgeous courts and mosques, I reflected on how much they had in common with the adjacent Wailing Wall, even apart from the fact that each of their custodians jealously guarded access to them. In many ways one would think they had nothing in common. On the one hand, rich courts, glorious color, functioning religious buildings with worshipers within. On the other hand, an (admittedly large) fragment of old scarred wall, a heartrending reminder that the building it once protected is now gone. Muslims may enter the still-standing mosques; Jews must stand and lament the loss of a temple no one has entered for almost two thousand years.

Yet despite these contrasts, the two sites have this in common: they are still merely places for believers to stand and send up prayers, offering their hopes to God like the tiny slips of paper folded up and shoved into the cracks of the Wailing Wall. The church I left that morning was different. For that building was not simply a place to come and pray and be safe from falling rain. It was a place where grace was even now being visibly and tangibly poured out.

The Wall, The Dome, and The House

Here then is the basic difference between modern Judaism and Islam on the one hand, and Christianity on the other: in Christianity alone one can come and find daily miracles, a place where God is not simply up above, the distant recipient of prayer offered at a wall or in a mosque, but here with us now, sacramentally and miraculously. In Christ alone, God is with us, and He acts, and saves, and transforms, and heals. He is active here and now in our midst: changing bread and wine into His Body and Blood, using water to bestow forgiveness and new birth, giving holy fire to those who wait for Him every Pascha, and pouring out His grace.

In this last example, I am not being merely poetic. For that very morning, at the Church of the Holy Sepulcher, we came once more to the Stone of Anointing and found it wet with myrrh. It was fragrant enough every time we had been there—so fragrant that people were spreading cloths upon it to soak up the myrrh and preserve the blessing. But this Sunday I found the myrrh so thick that it filled one of the little cracks in the slab, and I could submerge the end of my finger in it. Here is a miracle, a true outpouring of grace—and one that is available for everyone who comes, be they Christian, Jewish, Muslim, or anything else. Unlike the entry to the Temple Mount, here no one searched us for weapons. No one stood at the door telling people they could not enter unless they were Christian. Christ died for all, even for those standing and swaying at the Wailing Wall, even for those removing their shoes to enter their exclusive mosques, and every one of them was free to come and pray and find the bountiful, flowing grace.

The Stone of Anointing is the first thing one sees as one enters the Church of the Sepulcher, and I wonder if perhaps this is not why the Providence of God causes this stone to flow with myrrh, rather than the top of Golgotha or the Tomb. It must be daunting for a devout Muslim or a Jew to enter this place, for in this church they might feel very out of place. Yet here at the very door they would find a divine welcome—a fragrant gift, an outpouring of love. Such myrrh and love do not flow at the Wailing Wall, nor in the mosques of Temple Mount. They do flow here. Unlike the Wall and the Dome, this is not just a building. It is the true House of the living God.

Bethesda

The last place we visited before the end of our all-too-brief visit to the Holy Land was Bethesda. It is famous as the site of the Lord's healing of the paralytic. In John 5 we read that next to the Sheep Gate in Jerusalem a paralytic sat by a pool in Bethesda (probably from the Hebrew *beth chesed*, "house of mercy"), a building that had five porticoes or colonnades. The pool surrounded by these colonnades was periodically "troubled"—that is, the water within the pool bubbled, and many then thought this was caused by an angel, whose descent into the pool filled it with divine healing power. The first one into the pool after that, the story went, would soak up all the divine power and be healed of whatever sickness he had.

The paralytic had been afflicted for thirty-eight years—basically his whole adult life—and so he waited patiently by the poolside for the troubling of the waters. But his paralysis slowed him down too much, and whenever the water bubbled, someone always beat him into the pool.

Christ found him there and asked him, "Do you want to be healed?" The man was focused on the pool; he was obsessed with the pool. Possibly without taking his eyes off the water, he explained to Christ his problem, which was that he had no one to lift him into the pool in time.

But as it turns out, he didn't need the pool. All he needed was Jesus. The Lord told him to rise, take up his pallet, and go home. The man believed Jesus, "and immediately the man was made well, took up his bed, and walked" (John 5:9). The pool, of course, was not just a pool. For St. John telling the story, it was also an image of the Law, and the man an image of impotent Israel, long in weakness and affliction, trusting in the Law to help save them. But Israel didn't need the Law to save them. All they needed was Jesus.

I wanted to see that pool. It is beside the elegant Church of St. Anne and consists now of a series of excavations of immense complexity. Everything in the Holy Land has a long history, and it seems that in this case, all that history is present to the eyes of the tourist in a festive, chaotic jumble. I stared at the large ruins and had little idea of what it meant. It is certainly a complex series of layers, and I was grateful for the explanatory historical pamphlet St. Anne's Church provided. But even using the map on the pamphlet as I wandered in and out and around the ruins,

I still was not sure of what I was looking at. Layer after layer of history had jumbled it all up nicely. Scholars might be able to dope it out and read the map correctly, but not tourists or pilgrims. But somewhere down there, the miracle happened. I needed to step back spiritually and take it all in at a glance.

The history of the pool began with a large reservoir pool north of the city gates, the so-called upper pool. This fed the Temple with a water supply during the time of the first Temple (compare Is. 7:3). In the third century BC a second reservoir pool was added to increase the flow. It also became used for baths and a healing center.

It was here the sick would gather, hoping for a cure. Some scholars have suggested that in our Lord's day this was a pagan healing center, dedicated to a pagan god of healing—Serapis, or perhaps Asclepios. There was certainly a pagan shrine built over it in the time of Hadrian, after Jewish Jerusalem had been razed and a completely Gentile town built in its place, but other scholars have judged it was unlikely that such a pagan shrine would have been tolerated so close to the Temple in Jesus' day. And if Jesus' miracle took place in a fundamentally pagan environment, such an unusual occurrence surely would have provoked comment from John, especially since Jesus took care to work only among "the lost sheep of the house of Israel" (Matt. 15:24; 10:5–6). Given this determination, it seems unlikelier still that Christ would have entered a pagan shrine.

We may think therefore that Bethesda was a baths center just north of the Temple. As mentioned above, after the destruction of Jerusalem, Emperor Hadrian continued using it as a healing and therapeutic site, though of course invoking pagan gods. After Constantine began to change the world, a Byzantine basilica of immense size was built over the whole thing. After this was ruined, the Crusaders built a smaller chapel on its ruins. The present church of St. Anne was built next to it all later on. Now all that is left are the many layers of building and destruction and rebuilding in the courtyard below.

Once again the devotional heart searches in vain for the precise spot in which Christ found the paralytic. All we can know is that somewhere down there, through multilayered history laid bare by the patience of archeology, the sacred spot remains hidden, its exact location now known only by the angels. It was perhaps a fitting conclusion to my days in the Holy Land, for here in this tangle of stone and history is the tale of the Holy Land summed up and displayed. Those innocent of history may want to disembark onto Palestinian soil and come to the place of miracle, and find everything just as it was when the wonder occurred. We want to come to Bethesda, brush past the Church of St. Anne's haunting beauty, and find the exact bit of stone (conveniently marked by the Franciscans) on which the paralytic lay before Christ told him to pick up his pallet and leave. We long to see the Bethesda sanctuary just as it was when the paralytic first left it, its five stately porticoes still standing to welcome the next group of sick, who still wait by the waters.

It taxes our piety and our imagination to come and see a confusing pile of masonry where we cannot easily discern a great Byzantine basilica from a more modest Crusader chapel. But so it is. Our knowledge of history, both ecclesiastical and secular, might stop with the first century, but history itself keeps its relentless pace. It challenges and disturbs us when we disembark and wander the Holy Land. But as these pages have said over and over, that is all the more reason to remember that God is not found in the past. He is found by those who seek Him in the present hour. The paralytic discovered that looking back to the past, to the pool, was no solution. Christ offered him life as a gift in the present hour. He trusted Christ, took up his pallet, and found out that now is the acceptable time, now is the day of salvation. A careful and reverent study of the past should lead us to find that salvation in the present day.

CONCLUSION

Retaining the Rock

> *Some time after that, since it was already three full years since my arrival in Jerusalem, and I had seen all the places which were the object of my pilgrimage, I felt that the time had come to return in God's Name to my own country.*
>
> EGERIA, CHAPTER 17,
> AS SHE LEFT JERUSALEM

As the sun set on Sunday night, my traveling companion and I prepared to leave Jerusalem. We would have to catch a midnight taxi to reach Tel Aviv in the middle of the night for our early-morning flight next day, and we decided to leave plenty of time for the stinging gauntlet that is Israeli airport security. (It was a wise decision: a security man X-rayed and pawed through my friend's backpack four times, and checked with his superior to see if my friend was allowed to keep a fez he had bought for his child. A gauntlet indeed. They mostly left me alone, possibly thinking I looked too tired to be dangerous.)

On the long trip back, I had plenty of time to process all that we had seen and done in the last happy and chaotic eight days. I settled back in the airplane seat and closed my eyes. I thought if I listened very, very carefully, I could hear the quiet challenge of Gregory of Nyssa, asking, "So what was that all about? So many miles, so much effort and time—for what? What did you hope to find there? What *did* you find?" They are good questions, and I suspect I will be answering them for years to come.

The first thing I found was an added dimension of depth to my previous years of Scripture reading. It was as if I had been watching a movie on television, with the focus just a bit off and the image a bit blurry. Then someone twisted the knob and adjusted the set, and everything came into clearer focus. It was not that I couldn't see the picture before; it was just that now I could see more clearly.

This showed itself in ways too small and numerous to count: the size of the Old City walls, the actual distance between Golgotha and the Tomb, the distance and depth across the Kidron Valley, the distance from the Old City to Gethsemane, the location of the pool north of the city where the Assyrians challenged Hezekiah. None of this changed my textual exegesis.

But it changed my emotional exegesis. And for someone who lives to read the Bible, this was no small gift.

Secondly, I saw from afar and tasted the miracle that was Byzantium. I say *"was* Byzantium" and not "is," for though the Orthodox delight in the glory days when the double-headed eagle flew over the world, and though we still reflexively call Istanbul "Constantinople," those glory days have long gone. It is easy for moderns to disdain the Byzantines (or "the Romans," to use their own self-designation), and for many the term *byzantine* is synonymous with labyrinthine complexity and deceitful treachery. For many, even for many Orthodox, it now simply means "Greek."

But that is a diminution of what Byzantium offered the world, and even a distortion of it. For Byzantium was not simply the empire of the Greeks, but the commonwealth of Rome, a place where all languages and cultures could find a home and even supply an emperor (as many cultures and regions did). But more than simply a commonwealth, it was a vision. As we try to appreciate the glory of that vision, it is well to remind ourselves of how different that vision is from our own ideas of church and state, and of how that Byzantine state came about.

Our modern North American insistence on "the separation of church and state" (whatever that phrase might mean) does not position us well to appreciate Byzantium. We North Americans think inevitably in terms of checks and balances, rights and freedoms. The Byzantines were not unaware of these political realities (after all, they managed to survive as an empire for more than a thousand years), but these were not the things uppermost in their minds.

What was uppermost was the glory of God. They saw man not primarily as a political animal, but as a child of God, as someone destined to outlive this age with its politics and inherit the age to come. It was not the flag that held the greatest sanctity for them, but the Cross. For the Byzantines, everything reached its highest state of perfection when it gave glory to God—whether it were a man, a family, a nation, or an empire. Caesar could prosper and endure only with the help of God, and God gave that help to those who strove to do His will. The proverb "Righteousness exalts a nation, / But sin is a reproach to any people" (Prov. 14:34) came as no surprise to them. Their stated aim was not doing the will of the people or the majority of the people, but doing the will of the God.

Because of their commitment to the will of God, the images of that divine will abounded: icons were placed prominently in public buildings and God's aid was publicly invoked by the Church in her liturgies. The emperor sought to prostrate himself and his empire before Christ, and cultural signs of that prostration could be seen everywhere. That was the ultimate meaning behind all those big churches the imperial generosity built throughout the world. That was why Jerusalem and Bethlehem and the Mount of Olives and other lesser places were graced with basilicas.

Retaining the Rock

We take pluralism for granted, with its live-and-let-live approach to religion. The Christians prior to the birth of Byzantium experienced precious little of that live-and-let-live pluralism from the pagan Roman State. No one in power wanted them to live and thrive. Indeed, the law explicitly stipulated "Christians may not exist," and worshipping at the Christian Eucharist was a capital offense. The Church before Constantine was a catacomb church, in that Christians more often than not were forced to hide in the dark like men already dead.

The pagans walked in the light, boasted, strutted, fed their pagan deities through state-funded worship, and blasphemed the Christian God. The Jews, a protected minority and very powerful in the days of Constantine, and even a lifetime later in the days of St. John Chrysostom, also knew how to pull strings and to strut. The Christians could only hide and be humble, and when they spoke publicly it was either quietly or nervously. The Cross on which their Savior died lay forgotten in a cistern, its glory unrecognized by the world. The Christians who loved the Cross had no glory either. And so they thought it would be forever, until the end of time.

And then the unthinkable happened: The emperor himself began to favor the hunted Christians. The first thing he did was to call off the hunt. And then he returned the property of the hunted that had been wrongly confiscated. And then, even more startlingly, he began to talk like a Christian, and to ask for the favor and help of the Christian God, and to build

Him churches. It seemed like a dream. People who had, a few short years before, been persecuted by Diocletian looked at Constantine as if he were a sort of walking miracle. Christians, culturally speaking, came out of the shadows, blinking in the unaccustomed light.

That is the real meaning of the Church of the Resurrection (or to use its later name, the Church of the Holy Sepulcher). Just as Empress Helena's engineers providentially found the cross where it lay rotting in a cistern near Golgotha and brought it out into the light, where it could be adorned and honored by all the world, so her son Constantine brought the Church out of the catacombs into the light, where it could be adorned and honored by all the world. He built a church complex over the sites of the Lord's Cross and Tomb that amazed the world and amazed the Christians who worshipped in it most of all.

Constantine's engineers chipped around the rock to isolate the Lord's Tomb, chipped around the hill of Golgotha with its sloping incline, and built next to them a huge basilica. When the Christians held services to celebrate the anniversary of its dedication ever afterward in mid-September, they could think of no other scripture to describe this miracle than the prophecy of Isaiah 60:11–16, where God promises that He will beautify the place of His sanctuary and make the place of His feet glorious. "Also the sons of those who afflicted you / Shall come bowing to you, / And all those who despised you shall fall prostrate at the soles of your feet; / And they shall call you The City of the LORD, / Zion of the Holy One of Israel" (v. 14). It was time for the Christians to arise and shine, for their light had come.

Sadly, this light has been long extinguished, and Christian Zion now languishes in the dark as before. Things have come full circle in the inscrutable will of God, and those who once came bending low now have risen up and oppress once again. All is now in ruins, ruins that lie throughout the Holy Land to be dug up with the patience of the archeologist's trowel. Christians in the Holy Land have fallen on hard times, and many are leaving if they can. Those hard times are manifest in the necessity of drawing tourists to survive, of trading on their piety, and of offering supposedly authentic sites to the pilgrims even if they have little authenticity to offer.

Many people look at the spectacle that is the Church of the Holy Sepulcher and the other sites and see only something tawdry and fake. Tawdriness and fakery of course exist in the Holy Land, but they should be regarded not as a sin, but as an affliction. Survival is hard for Christians now in that land, and rival churches in Kefr Kenna each display waterpots to tourists, claiming that theirs is the authentic one. Things were not always this bad. Once they held their heads up high, and sang to God as a mighty multitude, and marched with banners under the sun. Their light has been badly eclipsed, through no fault of their own. But I have seen what that light meant once to the world, and that it was bright indeed. I have seen Byzantium under the ruins.

Thirdly, I have reached through the long past and touched the memorials of things more precious than life itself. That past was shrouded in darkness, so that I have needed the help of historians and scholars and archeologists to direct my hand and tell me where to reach—"not this place, but that one, not over there, but over here." I needed their aid to love God with all my mind (Mark 12:30), but it is the heart and the emotional center that feeds on the past. Like Egeria and others before me, I have come to the Holy Land hungry to connect with events of the past and to feed my piety on the things I have read in the Bible and pictured in my mind.

This is a murky and mysterious desire and one that defies easy analysis. It is summed up for me by a rock that I retain and that is for me a symbol of my entire pilgrimage. While we were at the Lake of Galilee, after I rolled up my pant legs and dipped my feet in the water, I selected a small rock from the sea that had been washed by the same water in which I had washed. I put it in my pocket and took it all the way home with me to Canada. It sits now in my office, looking to the unsuspecting like an ordinary paperweight. But to me it is not simply a paperweight. To me it is a bridge, a small stone connection to an experience in the Holy Land and, through that experience, a connection to sacred history.

What was the point of taking such a corny thing, following in the dubious footsteps of every other visitor to the Sea of Galilee? It was not that I couldn't have remembered that day without the visual aid of the rock. That day is one I will carry with me to the end of my life, with or without the rock. But we are physical animals, creatures of touch and sight as well as of memory and thought. God Himself seems to condescend to such frailty and saves us by sacraments instead of by syllogisms. And the rock is, if not sacramental, at least of sacramental tangibility.

We remember when our memories are jogged, and they are jogged by tangible things—by scents, by photographs, by school mementos. Even by rocks. The rock I retained from the Sea of Galilee is a chain, and by holding it I connect with everything else at the other end of that chain—not just my time by the Sea of Galilee, but everything else that happened in sacred history by that sea. Holding this rock, I am connected to Galilee's shore in the time of Christ and to the boats that pushed off from the shore, including Peter's boat carrying the Lord. I am connected to their miraculous catch of fish on the waters, to the miracle of Peter walking on the waters, to our Lord stilling its stormy waves. I am connected even to the part of Galilee's shore we cannot precisely identify today, the place where He had breakfast with His disciples after He was raised from the dead. All these things are held together as by a single chain, and I grasp that chain when I hold the rock.

That is the reason pilgrims have continually taken what some call mementoes from their trips to the Holy Land. They are not simply souvenirs, like the toys and T-shirts and coffee cups purchased in airport shops. Those truly are mere souvenirs and can be given to anyone as gifts and trinkets. Their connection with the sacred events is arbitrary and distant. They share nothing with the sacred events apart from the fact that they have been purchased in the Holy Land.

It is otherwise with things that have actually touched the sacred places. These things become bridges and chains, things capable of linking us to the sacred places themselves. That is why the faithful spread cloths on the Stone of Anointing, or touch their baptismal crosses to the rock of Golgotha, or place them for a brief moment on the slab over the Lord's Tomb. To call the things that have touched the sacred places relics (or, if the lawyers prefer, secondary relics) is perhaps too much, for spiritual power lies not in them so much as in the holy places themselves. But even though the things that have touched the holy places are not relics strictly speaking, they still have power to link us to the past. In holding them we retain, even if faintly, the ability to jump over time and space. I will retain my rock. And I think Egeria would understand.

Yet for all this, I still hear after all the faint insistent questioning of Gregory of Nyssa: "But did you come back really changed? Surely it's all about holiness. Did you grow any holier for all your expended effort?" Obviously such a question is for others to answer, not for me—and possibly not for them either. God is the only true judge of our progress in holiness. And it is surely true—I'll grant Gregory this much—that holiness is not the special gift of the Holy Land. No one will find God there who did not carry Him with him in his heart when he arrived, and if God is not encountered at home, He is perhaps not any more likely to be found in Palestine. To meet God one needs a hungry and humble heart, not just an Israeli stamp in one's passport. Holiness is no easier to attain there than at home, to which St. Jerome would be the first to attest from his cave in Bethlehem. A trip to Israel is not a shortcut to the Kingdom. The advantage perhaps is that by feeding one's piety upon the holy places, one can return home better prepared to seek holiness here.

What then of those who cannot make the trip or may never get to walk as a pilgrim in the Holy Land? Are they somehow disadvantaged? Gregory would say no, and I think that here Egeria would not disagree. It is a great thing to travel through time and space and touch the sacred past in the Holy Land. But God is even greater, and He is not bound by time or space.

In this regard I remember some words spoken by Augustine's mother, Monica, to her newly converted and soon-to-be-famous son. They were returning from Italy to their home in North Africa. Along the way, Monica became ill with a fever, and her death seemed imminent. This was a great grief to her emotional son, who wanted to fulfill her wish of being buried beside her husband in North Africa. He was bitterly sorry that she must die and be buried in a strange land so far from home. His mother bade her son be at peace and bury her anywhere. "No place," she said, "is far from God."

Monica's final motherly counsel may direct us as well. God's hand is not shortened, His greatness not diminished. He can save and sanctify any who turn to Him with their whole heart, whether or not they can travel to the Holy Land. No place is far from God.

Materials Consulted

Bar-Am, Aviva, *Beyond the Walls: Churches of Jerusalem*, Jerusalem: Ahva Press, 1998.

Bible History Daily, "The House of Peter: The Home of Jesus in Capernaum?" *Biblical Archeology Review*, 03/29/2011, http://www.biblicalarchaeology.org/daily/biblical-sites-places/biblical-archaeology-sites/the-house-of-peter-the-home-of-jesus-in-capernaum/

Farmer, Leslie, *We Saw the Holy City*, London: Epworth Press, 1944.

Judge, Joseph, "This Year in Jerusalem," in *National Geographic*, Vol. 163, No. 4, April 1983.

Kesich, Veselin and Lydia, *Treasures of the Holy Land*, New York: SVS Press, 1985.

Laney, Carl J., "The Identification of Cana of Galilee," http://www.bibleplaces.com/Identification_of_Cana_of_Galilee,_by_J_Carl_Laney.pdf

Prescott, H.F.M., *Jerusalem Journey: Pilgrimage to the Holy Land in the Fifteenth Century*, London: Eyre & Spottiswoode, 1954.

Sabbagh, Karl, *Palestine: A Personal History*, New York: Grove Press, 2006.

Taylor, Joan E., "The Garden of Gethsemane: Not the Place of Jesus' Arrest," *Biblical Archeological Review*, www.bib-arch.org/online-exclusives/easter-03.asp.

Theosophical Ruminations, "Biblical Archeology 38: Peter's House in Capernaum," http://theosophical.wordpress.com/2011/09/16/biblical-archaeology-38-peter%E2%80%99s-house-in-capernaum/.

Wilken, Robert L., *The Land Called Holy*, New Haven: Yale University Press, 1992.

Wilkinson, John, *Jerusalem as Jesus Knew It*, London: Thames and Hudson, 1978.

Wilkinson, John, *Egeria's Travels*, Warminster: Aris & Phillips Ltd., 1999.

About the Author

Archpriest Lawrence Farley currently pastors St. Herman of Alaska Orthodox Church (OCA) in Langley, B.C., Canada. He received his B.A. from Trinity College, Toronto, and his M.Div. from Wycliffe College, Toronto. A former Anglican priest, he converted to Orthodoxy in 1985 and studied for two years at St. Tikhon's Orthodox Seminary in Pennsylvania. He has published the books in the Orthodox Bible Study Companion series, as well as numerous other books including: *A Daily Calendar of Saints: A Synaxarion for Today's North American Church*; *Let Us Attend: A Journey Through the Orthodox Divine Liturgy*; *The Christian Old Testament: Looking at the Hebrew Scriptures through Christian Eyes*; *A Song in the Furnace: The Message of the Book of Daniel*; *Unquenchable Fire: The Traditional Christian Teaching about Hell*; *One Flesh: Salvation through Marriage in the Orthodox Church*; and *The Empty Throne: Reflections on the History and Future of the Orthodox Episcopacy*.

Listen to Fr. Lawrence Farley's podcast on Ancient Faith Radio

The Coffee Cup Commentary series provides studies in the Holy Scriptures, both Old and New Testaments. Many of the studies are taken from The Orthodox Bible Study Companion Series published by Ancient Faith Publishing.

www.ancientfaith.com

Also by
Lawrence R. Farley

A Daily Calendar of Saints
A Synaxarion for Today's North American Church
Popular biblical commentator and church historian Fr. Lawrence Farley turns his hand to hagiography in this collection of lives of saints, one or more for each day of the calendar year. His accessible prose and contemporary approach make these ancient lives easy for modern Christians to relate to and understand.

Let Us Attend!
A Journey through the Orthodox Divine Liturgy
A guide to understanding the Divine Liturgy and a vibrant reminder of the centrality of the Eucharist in living the Christian life. Every Sunday morning we are literally taken on a journey into the Kingdom of God. Fr. Lawrence guides in a devotional and historical walk through the Orthodox Liturgy. Examining the Liturgy section by section, he provides both historical explanations of how the Liturgy evolved and devotional insights aimed at helping us pray the Liturgy in the way the Fathers intended.

The Christian Old Testament
Looking at the Hebrew Scriptures through Christian Eyes
Many Christians see the Old Testament as "the other Testament": a source of exciting stories to tell the kids, but not very relevant to the Christian life. *The Christian Old Testament*

reveals the Hebrew Scriptures as the essential context of Christianity, as well as a many-layered revelation of Christ Himself. Follow along as Fr. Lawrence Farley explores the Christian significance of every book of the Old Testament.

A Song in the Furnace
The Message of the Book of Daniel
The Book of Daniel should be read with the eyes of a child. It's a book of wonders and extremes—mad kings, baffling dreams with gifted interpreters, breathtaking deliverances, astounding prophecies—with even what may be the world's first detective stories added in for good measure. To argue over the book's historicity, as scholars have done for centuries, is to miss the point. In *A Song in the Furnace*, Fr. Lawrence Farley reveals all the wonders of this unique book to the receptive eye.

Unquenchable Fire
The Traditional Christian Teaching about Hell
The doctrine of hell as a place of eternal punishment has never been easy for Christians to accept. The temptation to retreat from and reject the Church's traditional teaching about hell is particularly strong in our current culture, which has demonstrably lost its sense of sin. Fr. Lawrence Farley examines the Orthodox Church's teaching on this difficult subject through the lens of Scripture and patristic writings, making the case that the existence of hell does not negate that of a loving and forgiving God.

The Empty Throne
Reflections on the History and Future of the Orthodox Episcopacy
In contemporary North America, the bishop's throne in the local parish stands empty for most of the year. The bishop is

an honored occasional guest rather than a true pastor of the local flock. But it was not always so, nor need it be so forever. Fr. Lawrence Farley explores how the Orthodox episcopacy developed over the centuries and suggests what can be done in modern times to bring the bishop back into closer contact with his flock.

One Flesh
Salvation through Marriage in the Orthodox Church
Is the Church too negative about sex? Beginning with this provocative question, Fr. Lawrence Farley explores the history of the Church's attitude toward sex and marriage, from the Old Testament through the Church Fathers. He persuasively makes the case both for traditional morality and for a positive acceptance of marriage as a viable path to theosis.

The Orthodox Bible Study Companion Series
This commentary series was written for the average layperson. Working from a literal translation of the original Greek, the commentary examines the text section by section, explaining its meaning in everyday language. Written from an Orthodox and patristic perspective, it maintains a balance between the devotional and the exegetical, feeding both the heart and the mind.

Three Akathists:
+ Akathist to Jesus, Light to Those in Darkness
+ Akathist to the Most Holy Theotokos, Daughter of Zion
+ Akathist to Matushka Olga Michael

For complete ordering information, visit our website: store.ancientfaith.com.

Ancient Faith Publishing hopes you have enjoyed and benefited from this book. The proceeds from the sales of our books only partially cover the costs of operating our nonprofit ministry—which includes both the work of **Ancient Faith Publishing** and the work of **Ancient Faith Radio**. Your financial support makes it possible to continue this ministry both in print and online. Donations are tax-deductible and can be made at **www.ancientfaith.com.**

To view other books by Ancient Faith,
please visit our website: **store.ancientfaith.com**

Bringing you Orthodox Christian music,
readings, prayers, teaching, and podcasts
24 hours a day since 2004 at
www.ancientfaith.com